REMEMBER

CHELMSFORD

between the wars ?

Edward Adams

Ian Henry Publications

ISBN 0 86025 514 X

Published by
Ian Henry Publications, Ltd.
20 Park Drive, Romford, Essex RM1 4LH
and printed by
Gomer Press, Llandysul, Ceredigion SA44 4QL

THE THIRTIES - LNER TO BROOMFIELD

"Oh yes, I went through there once, on a day trip to Clacton," was the sort of remark a stranger would make, when he had asked where you lived, probably following up with, "Isn't it near Colchester?"

Chelmsford had a population of 26,000 in the thirties and, despite the presence of three major industrial companies; the town was not very prominent. The fact that it was the County Town of Essex and Marconi made the first broadcast from there, seldom made the borough hit the headlines, so we enjoyed a quiet life!

Anyone who recalls those far off days would assure you of one thing - it was possible to walk through High Street on a Saturday and meet several people you knew. Just being a Chelmsfordian was pleasurable. There were good, old-fashioned shops, with polite staff and, in many instances, the owner himself there to serve you. We had four cinemas, several parks, practically full employment and annual events that made life very happy.

Sadly, many familiar names above those shops, along with the proprietors, have long gone. But that is to be expected; the post-war years have seen rapid changes. Let's take a walk through the old town, starting at Martin's grocers, on the corner of Broomfield Road...

But first, glance across to the other side of Duke Street at the floral display and small lawn, surrounded by a low wire fence, outside Rainsford House, the red brick front wall of which was covered in evergreen creeper. This was the Borough Council office, sufficient in size for the population at the time, when Mr George Barford was town clerk. Between that and Dr Newton's house, with a garden and tall trees, which extended to the corner of Fairfield Road, the stark white stone memorial '*TO THE MEN OF CHELMSFORD WHO FELL IN THE GREAT WAR, 1914-1918*', rose from the pavement. At the far end of Fairfield Road, past several houses, was the office and yard of builder Henry Potter, who built Baddow Hall Estate. Eastern National bus station is referred to on page 38.

Back to Martin's - next door came Bellamy's chemists, then Hawkes confectioners, a ladies' hairdresser and Duke Street sub-post office, which was also a baker's shop, run by the Misses Shedd. Both Rippon's and Cramphorn's once had branches just here, so did Mrs Turner, a draper. Then came Mr C J Gramlick's jewellers, where he was ready in person, to serve or advise.

W & O Budd, bakers and confectioners were before the next group of shops, which were set back from the others, allowing the first, Harvey's Florists, plenty of room to display flowers outside. Beside them, Baxfield's fishmongers then bearded Mr Harry Hoy's tobacconist shop. Finally, before some private houses converted to offices, came Mr Jack Payne's photography business, under the name of E Nixon Payne, then Armstrong chemists and Archer's butchers. Before some of those mentioned here, other businesses once occupied the shops. Next to the PO, Mr Shedd ran a greengrocery; there was Coppin, a pork butcher, Rolph, newsagents and Fairhead's fishmongers.

On the corner of narrow Wells Street was Hugh Wright's, although along the front of this butcher's, with layers of sawdust covering the floor and treading out on to the pavement, was the name 'Underwoods', in large, embossed copper lettering. All children passing by loved to walk along and jump off the little platform, surfaced with glass tiles, which fronted the shop. Jovial Mr Wright, who was mayor several times, from 1925 to 1928 and 1932 to 1934, also owned other branches and would yearly attend the Smithfield Show in London, to purchase the prize beast, before it was slaughtered and sold as prime British beef for Christmas.

Curries was next door - there were several fruiterers in the town, privately owned, offering plenty of choice, well before the invasion of supermarkets. Traditional shoe shop, Finch's came next; there was a dry cleaners, Newcombe's cycle shop, yet another butchers and Bluebird restaurant, once owned by Leonard Monk, then by Chris Verdult, who, like Hugh Wright, became Chelmsford's mayor. Finally, on this side, the Plough public house, with a yard at the back where it was safe to leave a bicycle, while commuting to London by train. We didn't need anti-theft devices then.

Below the dark arches of the railway station, there was always a fishy smell, arising from the wooden boxes of fresh fish arriving by train every day, either from Harwich or Billingsgate. There were two booking office windows in the brown panelled woodwork extending from the doorway to the foot of the stairs leading to the up-line platform (to London), although usually just one was open, where passengers queued to purchase either first, second or third class tickets - train compartment doors were marked 1, 2 or 3. W H Smith's bookstall was just a trestle table, piled with daily newspapers and there was also a penny slot machine for obtaining a white platform ticket, essential for people wishing to see someone off.

Upstairs on the platforms were two more machines, one dispensing Nestlés penny chocolate bars. The other was a wide, impressive green and red contraption on which it was possible to obtain, for twopence, an embossed aluminium strip with letters and figures - for instance, one's name and address - achieved by moving a pointer and pressing a lever.

A familiar sight, when waiting on the station, was of a man walking on the track beside a train which was stationary by the opposite platform, carrying a long handled hammer and tapping every wheel, listening for signs of cracks. Our section of the railway system was run by LNER, known jokingly as Late & Never Early! The thirty mile journey to London took an hour and passengers arriving at Liverpool Street were accustomed to black surfaced platforms and a wide noisy station, with trails of baggage trucks winding their way among pedestrians and heaped boxes, while smoke and steam rose to the glass roof from oily green engines.

Facing the station forecourt in Duke Street was Clark's, a small office under a railway arch, where coal could be ordered. From late afternoon, newspaper sellers stood by to offer three evening papers, just arrived from London - *Standard, News* and *Star*, all at one penny each. One well-known character, 'Snowy' (whose nickname matched his hair) had one leg and would hop across the road, dodging traffic, when he spotted a customer.

Now let's return again to Martin's grocery, mentioned earlier. The store extended along Broomfield Road, taking in numbers two to six, with baker J W Thompson (later Wood's) next to it. After a fruit shop, confectioner and tailor, came another grocer, W J Payne, which was to become W J Johnson, on one corner of Railway Street, the Ship Inn being on the other corner.

There were mostly private houses, interspersed with an occasional business along this stretch, past Glebe Road, to Dr Martin's home, on the corner of Rectory Lane, Mr C E Ridley DL, JP, residing in the house on the opposite corner. A cream painted wooden house which once stood next door was actually a relic of old Chelmsford - it was part of the first railway station and was moved to this location when the more substantial building was erected.

A short distance down Rectory Lane, on the left side, was a grey stone wall and archway leading into the Friends' Burial Ground and a little further on; a busy general store was a draw for workers needing sweets and cigarettes. Occupying several acres off Rectory Lane and New Street was the Hoffmann Manufacturing Company's ball and roller bearing factory - more of this later.

Back to Broomfield Road - the Keene Memorial Homes, for elderly people, were a gift from Miss Lavinia Keene, of Galleywood, in memory of her late husband, John Henry. They were built in the mid-thirties next to the County High School for Girls, where Miss E M Bancroft was the highly respected, but very strict headmistress for many years. She taught 'scripture' to some classes but when she set homework, detailing chapter and verse what she wanted them to read, the girls didn't bother to do it, because she would always go through it carefully in the next lesson! Another subject, taught at the school in the twenties was home nursing, though any talk about blood would make some girls feel faint!

High School uniform then included a navy blue serge tunic with three box pleats at the front up to a square neck, over a long sleeved white blouse and a matching blue necktie. A peculiar hat, to be worn to and from school was tight fitting over the forehead with a brim anchored each side by a small strap, causing the sides to point out. On the front was a white embroidered badge. By the end of the thirties, berets were worn and the uniform had been modernised to navy skirt and blazer over a white blouse.

Several large private houses along here were the homes of local business people, including Fred Luckin Smith, G C Blooman (of Bond's) and the Misses Marriage, whose adjoining residences were, by 1938, St John's Maternity Home. The Avenues, from First to Seventh, were built in the thirties; mainly by Wade's and Mr Wade himself lived in Broomfield Road, next to the Hiner family, between Third and Fourth Avenues.

On the other side of Broomfield Road (designated a Roman Road on some old maps), a large house, Brownings, stood well back, hidden by high hedges and when Boarded Barns Estate had been built on farm land in the mid-twenties, the second turning off the new Kings Road was named Brownings Avenue. Behind the house and next to a defunct pottery, were wireless masts belonging to a Marconi Signal Station. Further along the main road, on this side, just around the corner of Patching Hall Lane, Patching Hall Farm buildings were on the right hand side.

Returning towards town along Broomfield Road, other notable buildings or businesses, after Christy Bros., which was on one corner of King's Road, included a Gospel Hall, Compasses Inn, Crisp the baker, decorator A J Cawley and Holmes builders' yard, opposite the Keene's Homes. One day the latter site became a petrol station, while builder Don Holmes himself continued to live in Swiss Avenue, not very far away.

King Edward VI Grammar School, which extended almost from there to Cedar Avenue and was first established in The Friars in 1551, is the subject of the final chapter.

Few people could ever have imagined the tremendous changes that would take place in this end of town by the turn of the century.

Chelmsford Cathedral

THE TWENTIES - BUFFALO BILL TO NITTY NORA

"What is the first thing you remember?" a psychiatrist friend once asked me, expecting an immediate reply.

It was very easy to answer - in 1927, when nearly three, I saw a white horse emerge through the open gate of a field opposite my home, 2 Lady Lane (now number 5) and race down Manor Road. It was heading for the council depôt, where, each day, it was harnessed to a dustcart. But it should not have escaped from the field, adjacent to R H Currie's farm - and that vision has remained with me throughout my life.

During that era, dustcarts were open topped and a dustman came round to the back of each home, carrying a skip. He would tip the contents of the dustbin into his skip - scattering ashes from coal fires on the path - and, slinging the skip on his back, return to the cart. Mounting a wooden step at the side, he tipped the rubbish into the vehicle: not very hygienic, but perfectly acceptable at the time. When dustcarts became motorised, they were no longer open topped, but had four steel lids along each side and as the dustman stepped up on a lever, the lid opened for him to tip in the contents of his skip.

The council tip was in former gravel pits, behind houses in what was colloquially known as The Stomps, a gravel track, later named Longstomps Avenue. In the twenties there were just a few houses on the left side, leading up to a cornfield at the top end and in that field, as in other similar fields on the edge of town, a yearly ritual was the killing of rabbits at harvest time. As corn was cut, the frightened animals gradually retreated to the remaining standing stalks, until there was no more cover in which to hide. Then the waiting crowd of men, women and children set to work, striking the unfortunate creatures, as they emerged, with heavy sticks, to provide themselves with a tasty meal.

My brother Doug, was a pupil at The Friars School, in a short thoroughfare between Lower Moulsham and London Road, but my sister, Dorrie, attended Trinity Road School, which she walked to and from each day, and also came home to lunch, too, though she did have a two-hour break for it. There were no short cuts - she walked down Mildmay Road into Baddow Road, then Moulsham Street and High Street and along Springfield Road until turning up Trinity Road, just past the end of Victoria Road.

That field where the horse was stabled, bordered on one side by Lady Lane and adjacent to Bouverie Road has since had many dwellings built on it, but once, prior to the twenties, the great American showman, Buffalo Bill (Colonel Cody) had brought his touring Wild West show to perform there.

Shortly after the incident with the white horse, my family moved to Park Avenue, Rainsford End, and my brother was one of the first pupils at the new Kings Road School, while my sister was by then at the High School in Broomfield Road.

As was customary with many pre-school children, during cold weather I wore leather, knee-length gaiters, fastened down one side with a row of buttons, necessitating the use of a buttonhook. A Liberty bodice, often referred to nowadays as a joke item by comedians, was another essential piece of clothing, worn as a vest and secured with a row of buttons at the front.

I suffered from what were termed the 'usual childhood ailments'. As did most children – chicken pox, measles and mumps. There was no panic, we justr accepted them as part of growing up and inoculations were not even considered. Extra casre was taken to protect the eyes from strong light when we had measles, but othyerwise the diseases were considered to be nature's way of immuning us from suffering from them later in life.

On reaching my fifth birthday, I too went to King's Road, my teachers being Miss Dick and Miss Read, who insisted that children who wrote with their left hand must change to the right. The formidable headmistress, Miss Wadley would often be seen gripping a boy's chin firmly in one hand and exclaiming, "Tiresome boy."

For a ha'penny, we could buy a third of a pint of milk, in a bottle sealed with a wide cardboard lid. At playtime, we would drink the milk after pushing a straw through a central perforation in the cardboard. A few children collected the lids, threading them on string.

One artistic teacher drew a colourful Hiawatha scene in chalk, which remained for some while on a blackboard and she also organised a class band, in which pupils could 'graduate' from playing triangle to drum! But on moving up to 'the big boys', we encountered a stricter regime. Teachers expected a rap and us to obey them instantly over the knuckles by shortish Mr Jones with the wooden back of a blackboard cleaner or on the open palm with a ruler were regular punishments.

The four school houses were named after Antarctic explorers, Scott, Oates, Evans and Shackleton. In class, we had double desks, sitting side by side with another pupil, each with an inkwell to dip in our pens.

The whole school was built around a grass quadrangle, Boys on the right hand side, Girls opposite, separated by Infants, the hall and offices plus main entrances making up the fourth side. The boys' toilets were outside, across the playground.

Mr Corey was so impressed by my older brother's progress, that when I eventually came into his class and he felt that my work was not up to standard, he once made me fetch my brother from the top class to see my 'terrible' work! How humiliating! All boys who, at age eleven had not passed the entrance exam ('the Scholarship') to the Grammar School left at the age of fourteen and the same rule applied, of course, to pupils in the adjoining girls' school, who had the opportunity to go on to the High School.

There was never any mixing with the Girls' School, not even on special occasions. They did not have their own assembly hall or join in morning prayers with the boys. Headmistress was Miss Mellor and teachers Miss Cook or Miss Armitage would punish talking in class with a rap on the hand with a ruler. School houses were Mary Slessor, Florence Nightingale, Grace Darling and Edith Cavell - all illustrious women.

In my class photograph, dated 1933, Mr J H Tremear appears, standing beside his fifty pupils, which was then the standard number in a class. Some boys knew him as 'Slipper', because his method of punishment was a whack on the behind with a plimsoll. Headmaster was Alec O Moon, who once caned me for cycling in the playground. Music teacher F R Billington taught us mostly sea shanties and traditional English folk songs. He lived to a ripe old age, still playing the organ in his local church.

J H Tremear and his 1933 class

Other teachers included tall and likeable Mr Tappenden; dapper Mr Tarrant; Mr Marsh, whose son was in my class and Leonard F Clist, who suffered from Great War shellshock and was unfortunately teased by some older boys. An abiding memory is his account of the many years before, when men working in Chelmsford Cathedral neglecvted to shore up a pillar, causing the whole building to come crashing to the floor. A young student teacher, Mr Hymas came to the school for a while, and then went on to join the staff at the new Moulsham Schools, off Princes Road.

Having learned about Adam being the first man on earth, I naïvely believed that that was why my name always appeared first on the register. The illusion was shattered when a new boy joined the class - his name was Abrahams! A friend confessed he burst into tears on the way home, when carrying his term report, which was supposed to be handed unopened to a parent. He had peeped inside and seen the number 49, which he assumed was his position in class, but was in reality the total of boys then in the class.

We read *Treasure Island*, featuring Jim Hawkins; then *Tom Sawyer*, followed by *Huckleberry Finn*, always identifying with those young heroes. All of us collected cigarette cards, trying to complete sets of cricketers, railway engines or cars and also used them in a game, where one was leaned against a wall and 'flicked' with other cards, to knock it over.

It was such a rare occurrence at King's Road for boys to pass the scholarship, that a board, headed 'Roll of Honour' was displayed above the stage in the assembly hall, listing the four (including my brother) who had passed in previous years! Things had improved by the time my turn came and five of us were successful - but we never did find out whether our names were added to that board.

Every morning, we assembled in the hall for prayers by the Head and sang a hymn, accompanied on the piano by Mr Billington and, though very rarely, a boy who had committed a serious breach of school rules would be caned on stage. On November 11th, we gathered to observe two minutes' silence, the service from the Cenotaph relayed through a wireless. One year, during the silence, the whole country was horrified to hear a man shout, "Cease this hypocrisy." We were listening at the time and Mr Moon made a comment afterwards, attempting to explain the interruption.

A fellow pupil throughout my entire eleven years school career was Maurice Stedman, who lived in Woodland Road. He was a most unusual personality, did not mix and was hopeless at sport, being constantly teased. However, at the age of sixteen, his amazing photographic memory enabled him to sail through exams with ease, leading to his later becoming an Oxford professor, perhaps the only one of former Kings Road school pupils of those days to achieve this distinction.

Once a year, all classes received a visit from a cleric, presumably to check that we were receiving religious instruction. Sometimes Mr Shakeshaft, from North Avenue Congregational Church, opposite the school, came and on other occasions, it was Rev J H Morgan, vicar of the Parish. One of his two churches, All Saints was also across the road, behind The Barn public house. The other was St Peter's in Primrose Hill. Another regular visitor was District Nurse Nellie Levett, who examined our heads, looking for traces of fleas and then our teeth, while boys who had neglected to brush them could be seen frantically attempting to polish them with their fingers, before going before her! In today's parlance, she would have been 'Nitty Nora'!

A row of shops in King's Road, next to a piece of waste ground, included Co-operative grocers, where my mother shopped, always quoting her 'divi' number, 2729. Co-op butchers adjoined, then came R H Currie, greengrocer and lastly Wells, post office, stationers and confectioners. As Boat Race Day approached every March, 'favours' were on sale in the post office and we wore light or dark blue emblems on our lapels. Cambridge always seemed to be the winning crew.

But when a new row of shops was added in 1933, they brought much more variety to the parade. There was a greengrocer - competition for Currie's round the corner -Ted Rippingale, a barber, where boys had their hair cut for sixpence, as long as they didn't go on Saturdays, which were reserved for working men; Jarman's, a cycle and radio shop, where wet batteries for wireless sets (accumulators) were charged up - it was my job to take our battery there from home, in a wooden carrier made by my father, when the 'juice' was running low.

Last in the row came Sturgeon's, a real children's delight, displaying an exciting new array of chocolates and inexpensive sweets. Liquorice laces, chewy black-jacks, (four a penny), ha'penny tubes of Swizzels, gob-stoppers (which continually changed colour as they were sucked, but were too large to conceal in the mouth while in class!) and 'surprise packets', containing broken bits of ice wafer, a boiled sweet and 'toy'. There were not only the familiar yellow packets of Barrett's sherbet fountains, with liquorice tube in the top, but sherbet dabs - triangular paper packets of sherbet, with a toffee lolly you could suck and dip into the powder; on the shelves were rows of colourful glass jars, containing a wide variety of appetising confectionery. This very soon became the favourite shop, with Mr & Mrs George Sturgeon the kindly, popular proprietors.

George Sturgeon at the opening of his confectionery/tobacconist shop in King's Road in March, 1933

DUKE STREET AND OLD MARKET

Under a low arch next to the station booking hall, taxis queued for custom, while on the other side of the railway forecourt was Mr John Austin's County Motors impressive car showroom. This adjoined Hawkes, on the corner of Victoria Road, one of several shops owned by the local boiled sweets manufacturer. On the opposite corner, Dorset House, a dentist's surgery, was often a refuge on Fridays, when cattle were driven up Market Road (now Victoria Road South), across Duke Street and into Victoria Road, on their way to be loaded on to trucks in the railway goods yard. Several alarmed ladies would be seen taking sanctuary behind the high railings of the house, as the restless, wild-eyed animals galloped by.

Beside the Lion and Lamb was an off-licence and there was an entry to Rose Bros. garage, where their Daimler wedding cars were kept. A dress shop, entered up two steps adjoined Joseph Mason's bookshop, then came Cedar Café, owned by Percy Smith, who employed waitresses dressed in neat brown uniforms, serving delicious cream cakes. At Osborne's tobacconist, a little flame burned perpetually on the counter, while behind it sat the proprietor, continually smoking a pipe.

Through a passage was H G Shergold's, a popular printer who produced many programmes and tickets for local events and hand set large type to print posters. Frank Raven, a milliner, was next to A J Andrews' Funeral Furnishers, who also provided cars for weddings. One of their drivers, John Jordan, married one time Mayor Arthur Andrews' daughter, Peggy and, in due course, took over the business.

Macarthy's chemists adjoined no.17, Fred Taylor & Co, estate agents and valuers, presided over by tall Major Wilks, wearing his half frame spectacles. His son, Tony and daughter Mary later joined the firm. At the side of their ground floor office were double doors leading to a large room where household goods were regularly auctioned, pipe-smoking Frank Byford being auctioneer's clerk. Lending a willing hand at auction time were his assistant, George "showing here, sir" Harvey and florid faced Walter Harris, who owned a removals business, based in Broomfield.

Taylors employed young men who had not long left school as office clerks and rent collectors. In the latter capacity, they would regularly mount the firm's ancient black upright bicycle and ride around several residential streets, from Victoria Road to Upper Bridge Road, with a leather bag slung over the handlebars, containing money collected. This was not considered at all hazardous and the boys took the task in turns, as they also did in going by bus to Maldon, once a week, where rents were collected from two terraced rows of poor cottages known as The Downs. The tenants' toilets, which were wooden privvies in back gardens, were shared between two households and rents were no more than three shillings and sixpence per week.

As practised at many offices at the time, carbon copies of letters produced by Taylor's typist were daily placed in a large ledger, made of tissue paper pages that were then dampened. Pink blotting paper separated the pages. The book was put in a press, resulting in the carbon copy being transferred into the ledger, to provide a complete record of outgoing mail. A time consuming process for the office boy!

On the first floor was a small office that was the local branch of the mighty Eagle Star Insurance, staffed by just two people, manager Cliff Houghton and a typist. On the top floor was County Typewriting Office, where Miss Hilda Sorrell taught shorthand and typing. Being a first-rate typist, she was also much in demand for her ability to produce important and often complicated, legal documents for various offices. She had previously worked with Miss M E Cottee, who owned a similar agency across the road. Castle's (formerly Manning's) off-licence was next door and further along, Percy Fulcher, well-known florist was beside Dixon's, men's outfitters, owned by Alderman Dixon, which later became Margery Heard's dress shop.

After J Walter Slipper's estate agency, came the imposing jewellers, W G Webber, their large two-sided clock, an essential boon to many, protruding from an upper wall. The final shop, before Church Lane, a footpath to the Cathedral Hall, was heralded by a most appetising aroma, brought about by beaming Mr H J Harrison, as he roasted and ground coffee beans inside the window of his high quality grocers, all the time waving happily to passers by. A feature of this part of town, the blue smoke that curled from a little chimney drifted along the street, enabling that delicious fragrance to be detected some yards away.

Just behind was Mr A E Wiseman's architect's office. The open area in front of a red brick wall round this part of the cathedral churchyard eventually became a bus stop. Batson's, typewriter specialist was the next shop, then Scott's stationers and Ward's Bookshop, where chocolate was also on sale, from very obliging Mr Frank Ward. In the twenties, there had been very different businesses occupying these premises - a café, china shop and confectioner. Essex & Suffolk Insurance office was separated from the corner shoe shop of Amey & Cook by an open entrance to the rear of these premises and by Cobb & Wincer, Estate Agents, managed by George W Mather, who was also the honorary treasurer of Chelmsford Carnival Association.

Almost adjoining Wiseman's, along Church Walk was the Cathedral Hall, scene of so many activities, from jumble sales to concerts, amateur theatricals, various social events and as dressing rooms for large numbers of clergy occasionally attending Cathedral functions.

A rough path separated the Hall from James Macpherson, manufacturers of appetising ginger beer, which was sold in brown stone bottles. They were also based at Maldon and one day metamorphosed into the nationally known Britvic. Further along Cottage Place were the town telephone exchange and Girl Guides' hall and nearby, the small Cathedral School. Proceeding along the wall bordering the cathedral churchyard into New Street, various small shops were seen on both sides of the road.

A lady known as 'May' lived along here and was notorious for her habit of calling out to passing men folk, from an upstairs window. Hawkes Bros. factory opposite, employed several men who moulded and stretched layers of sugary concoctions to produce an assortment of highly coloured sweets and glucose barley sugar, to be packed by lines of ladies. Long established Hadler's Garage, close by, run by Bob Hadler and his father, was near the junction with Victoria Road.

Returning to Duke Street, opposite Cobbe & Wincer, was Chelmsford Corporation Gas showroom, where a distinct smell of gas was most noticeable when entering, probably caused by the use of gas lighting fittings, with which the shop was illuminated. Gas showrooms were the only outlets where one could legally buy an appliance, such as a fire or cooker and here it was also possible to pay bills. The most commonly seen cooker was of a make called 'Main' and we had one in our kitchen at home, coloured black with white enamelled door, edged in pale blue, which lasted for many years. We did not need to take out 'extended guarantees' in those days - goods were built to last.

Next door was H & T C Godfrey, makers and retailers of leather goods. A cleaners was between that and the Golden Fleece, with its suspended gold lamb sign, on the corner of narrow Threadneedle Street - a very short thoroughfare totally unlike its namesake in the City of London.

When County Hall was built in the thirties, partly on a site where there had been Parke's opticians, Flexman's radio shop and various offices, we marvelled at its nine-storey height! It could be seen from as far away as Danbury Common and overshadowed the line of solicitor's premises, extending along Duke Street as far as Dr Alford's house. To gain entrance to them all, one needed to climb well-worn white stone steps, a black wrought iron handrail being on one side. The doctor's walled garden extended down Market Road and his magnolia tree produces its glorious annual blossom to this day.

On the other corner of Market Road (Victoria Road South) was Mr Dannatt's architects' office, next to a most popular restaurant, Cannon's, owned by ebullient Mr Gilbert Wilcox, where many dances and private functions were held. Mr Wilcox's son, Bob, would eventually take over the business. A service road at the side separated this from The Friends' Meeting House, surrounded by trees. Finally, on the corner of Park Road, leading to the Recreation Ground was the Railway Tavern.

A walk down the right hand side of Market Road, first past Boatman's opticians (where one could purchase a camera for 17/6d in 1935), then Eastern Garages (which occasionally showed Morris car film programmes in the showroom) and the Baptist Church brought one to the town Library (in 1936 it became the Mid-Essex Technical College and School of Art) and a public right of way to Park Road. The Duchess of Gloucester, later Princess Alice, once could have been seen inspecting ranks of dark uniformed Red Cross personnel here. The Territorials' Drill Hall was at the bottom end and after a sharp turn to the left, the cattle market came into view.

On Fridays, market day, red painted pens enclosed sheep, cows, bullocks and pigs, while auctioneers worked their way along wooden walkways above them, taking bids from farmers. In covered areas were chickens, ducks and produce. The whole presented a satisfying and peaceful scene of country living around the County Town.

Next to the market was the town fire station, at the side of which another short length of Threadneedle Street led to the wrought iron gated entrance to 'The Rec', as our Recreation Ground was known, half a dozen cottages being on the right hand side, backing on to the firemen's yard, which housed their tall drill tower, used for hanging fire hoses and rescue practice.

Tindal Square was presided over by an impressive statue, erected in 1851, in honour of Judge Nicholas Conyngham Tindal, one of the town's most famous sons, who was born in Moulsham Street in December 1776 and in due course became Lord Chief Justice. His great-uncle John and great-grandfather Nicholas had both been headmasters at King Edward VI School and he came to live at Coval Hall, grounds of which then adjoined the school. He was made Solicitor General in 1820, serving as MP for Harwich, and died in1846, leaving three children. His statue in the Square appeared to be green, but was actually bronze, covered in verdigris. It had a drinking water tap on one side of the white stone plinth, beneath which was a bowl for dogs. A separate stone horse trough was nearby.

Groups of farmers, grain merchants and millers would be seen chatting in the roadway outside the Corn Exchange, where many of them entered to buy and sell corn, from high desks set in long rows across the floor. This partly glass roofed, major building in the heart of town, saw many and varied activities. At one time, the mayor would declare election results from the outside balcony, to vociferous crowds gathered impatiently in The Square below.

The Chelmsford Society of Model Engineers exhibited there annually and every afternoon for several years, Bob, a newspaper seller, sat on a ledge at the front, offering three evening papers. All-in wrestling, WI conferences, bazaars and many other functions were held and a sixpenny 'hop' was a regular weekly dance, to the music of one of several local dance bands. Before the building was demolished, it was even used as a roller skating rink: Johnny Dankworth and Cleo Laine also appeared there.

The retail market was much smaller than that provided today. A triangular area behind the Golden Fleece, bounded by Market Road and Threadneedle Street was sufficient for several stalls and, as in all markets, there were some well-known characters. Among them was a man affectionately known as 'Ol' Miller', who sold towels, sheets and other linen items and regularly attracted a crowd of amused shoppers with his banter; Mr Escott sold polishes and soaps, including one named Zixt, which was gritty and ideal for removing grease from hands of Hoffmann workers, though some men preferred to use Vim, a scouring powder sold in yellow tubular shakers, also for sale on this stall. An elegant lady, who wore a fashionable hat, sat at her stall to sell a variety of jewellery; a purveyor of boiled sweets and chocolate was always busy serving eager buyers of his special deals and there was a man offering inexpensive curtain and dressmaking fabrics. When late afternoon winter darkness descended, stalls were illuminated by large oil pressure lamps that cast a yellow glow all around them.

Eastern National buses, which normally traversed from Tindal Square through Market Road, went instead via King Edward Avenue on Fridays, so as to avoid the cattle market, first passing, on the corner, J Brittain Pash, dealers in heavy machinery and other items essential to farmers, from chicken feeders to tractors. On the side of the Avenue backing on to County Hall were some Victorian private houses, converted into offices. One of the busiest of these was the Registrar, where one had to register births, marriages and deaths. This office had been relocated from a private house in Swiss Avenue, off Broomfield Road, the home of Mr Fred Turner, who, besides being Registrar, was also 'town vaccination officer'.

Basil Harrison and his coffee roaster

GIRAFFE NECKED WOMEN AND THE LAUGHING POLICEMAN

Amey & Cook's shoe shop, on Duke Street - Tindal Square corner, was beside a second Godfrey's, where a rich aroma of new leather was evident immediately one entered. Here were harnesses, horse brasses, commercial leather goods, ropes and canvas tents, much of which was made at their old established factory in Moulsham. Debnam's hairdressers, alongside, was popular with white collar workers in town and next door was one of the chemists run by the Bellamy family - as with some of the other locally owned businesses in Chelmsford, the proprietors held the office of Mayor at some time in their lives.

Balch & Balch estate office was on the corner of the main pathway to the west door of the cathedral - a very uneven surface of ancient paving stones, along which many newly weds have taken their first steps of married life and judges walked in procession before the opening of Assizes in the grand Shire Hall. Dominating High Street, the latter ancient building has hosted countless important functions within and on the steps outside, besides some famous trials and notable functions in the ballroom. Many boys, through the years, like me, clambered on top of the shiny black Sebastopol cannon on its mottled granite plinth in front of the Shire Hall and, sitting astride the huge barrel, 'aimed' it at the Corn Exchange. The gun, which had rested in this position since 1858 was moved into Oaklands Park, to face the museum, some years ago.

A touring exhibition held in the Shire Hall in April 1937 was a curious mixture. Sponsored by the *Daily Sketch*, it had two main attractions. Exact replicas of the entire collection of Crown Jewels were displayed in illuminated glass cases, glittering under spotlights, while three 'Giraffe Necked Women' were also there, on a dais. The three pretty young black ladies had their long necks covered in brass rings, placed there as part of tribal ritual and were described as being 'On Loan from Bertram Mills Circus'. The girls, Muklat, Muswaitha and Mutha, were pleased to give me their autographs. It is very doubtful whether such a display would be permitted nowadays.

Across the road, in New Street, Tindall & Jarrold bookshop was next to the police station, which, with G B Hilliard, market auctioneers, were either corner buildings of Waterloo Lane. At the far end were the borough's open-air swimming baths, enjoyed by young and old in summer and annually for school galas. However, some children found it advisable to wear socks in the water, to save them from slipping over on the slimy bottom.

The left hand side of the lane was occupied by the garden of Guy Harlings, residence of Canon W E R Morrow, a long serving Provost of the Cathedral. The Very Reverend's gardener, Mr Scarlet, wearing his customary battered trilby, could often be seen cutting the large lawns, smoke from his pipe competing with fumes from the motor mower! Main entrance to the big house was in New Street, Mr & Mrs Scarlet's picturesque cottage being beside it, a cobbled yard separating the two buildings.

On the right hand side of Waterloo Lane were the Post Office sorting depôt, mail van garage and Luckin & Sheldrake's three storey accountancy offices.

In the High Street, the General Post Office was between Hilliard's and Barclay's Bank, in which only a wide, dark polished counter separated customers from the staff - glass partitions were not considered necessary. My mother used to pay in my father's salary cheque there every Friday and draw out £5 in cash, which was sufficient for her to buy all our groceries, with a bit left over for clothing for us all.

The old coaching inn, Saracen's Head was next, then Miss Ashford's Tindal Café and Spalding's double windowed toy store, usually displaying Hornby model trains racing round a winding track. Many photos by Mr Fred Spalding (another former Mayor, his tenure in office being 1922-25) record the early 1900's history and personalities of the town, without which much of the Borough's past would have been lost to us. His shop naturally had to include a photographic studio.

A traditional event was the arrival at the store every year of Father Christmas, by 'sleigh', or open car, from the direction of the railway station, throwing little wrapped gifts to children as he passed through cheering crowds, before entering his grotto in the shop. This carried on a tradition first introduced by another old-established business, Bolingbroke's, who first brought the old gentleman to town in 1921.

Beside the toy store was red brick paved Crane Court, then came Wiseman's, draper and milliner, Westminster Bank, Freeman Hardy & Willis shoes, Saltmarsh florist's and the Misses Self & Hicks baby wear. There followed Parke's chemist's, Chapman's Jewellers, owned by Mr Bert Raven, Joseph Gripper ironmongers, where director Tom Merritt was often to be seen helping in the store, and E J Rippon, newsagents. There was a yard beside Gripper's, where they dealt in heavy materials for engineers, including the supply of sheet metal and chain.

Scotch Wool Shop and Cramphorn's seed merchants, with their Head Office situated above, were opposite London Road and Cramphorn family members were part of the work force. Ted Fairhead was the knowledgeable shop manager and one of the senior staff, portly Mr E R Cottam, also wrote a gardening column in the *Essex Chronicle*. Anyone entering those offices would have been aware that the ancient flooring was slanted in places, causing the wide, polished tables, used as desks by busy book-keepers, while entering their figures in heavy, leather bound ledgers, to slope at an alarming angle. From their long yard beside the shop, horse drawn carts would emerge, loaded with seed potatoes, straw and other produce, for distribution to customers.

Pausing for a moment here, we could often see the 'Laughing Policeman' - in reality, an ever-smiling, short Special Constable, who directed traffic at London Road corner in the High Street. He would point to a spot by him, inviting a driver to wait there before waving him on. Like a predecessor, he drew the occasional admiring crowd, to watch his antics and approve his good humour. He would often leave his position in the middle of the road, to move bicycles leaning on the curb that had impeded traffic in this narrow part of High Street.

The predecessor referred to was tall PC Baker, popularly known as 'Kruschen', implying that he must have taken Kruschen Salts in order to maintain his ultra smart, military bearing. Directing traffic on that corner, he used to keep his arms as straight as possible, his immaculate white gloves indicating only too clearly exactly what he expected drivers to do. In his later years, as a detective, he also had a reputation of solving crimes and, if 'Kruschen' was known to be on the case, people were confident that everything would soon be cleared up.

Leading from London Road, on the right hand corner of Tindal Street (also known as Back Street) was a little confectioners, kept by the Misses Caton. One of these sisters was a Sunday School teacher at St Peter's Church, Rainsford End. She wore her hair in 'earphones' and the dear ladies' shop was as old-fashioned as its proprietors. Imitation chocolate bars, colourful crêpe paper and artificial flowers decorated the low windows and there was one step down to enter, to be greeted by an enticing smell of sweets. Next door, Duncombe's, florists, was also down a step and through a low door. Both shops were demolished when London Road was widened.

In Tindal Street, an old part of town, were former coaching inns, with long back yards where stables used to be. At London Road end a cycle shop stood on the left corner (later to become Wainwright's Milk Bar), next to Mrs McNair, hairdresser and G B Ling, a bow windowed shop selling farm products and owned by Cramphorn's. A warm, countryside aroma of straw, seeds, corn and other chicken feed greeted one on entering, via three stone steps up.

On this side of the narrow street were Frank Poney, baker, the Dolphin and Spotted Dog inns, the latter, having three bow windows on the first floor, was managed by popular Mrs Cheyne. Many businesses here at the start of the thirties, including a shoemaker, draper and tailor, did not survive to the end of the decade. In their place came a café, Cook's off-licence and Pope and Smith, which not only purveyed equipment for all types of sporting activities, but was owned by the cousins Peter and Ray Smith, who played cricket for Essex (and Peter for England). Don Spencer, who became a director after Dudley Pope was killed in an accident, captained Essex second eleven and his brother Dick also worked at the shop. The business had been established in High Street in 1932.

A long established ironmonger, Hasler & Hance was one of the most well liked businesses in town. Often welcomed with a cheerful greeting, "Hullo old dear, now what can we help you with today?" from Stanley Hance, one of the two proprietors, customers might then experience a long wait, while their pane of glass or little piece of wire netting for a rabbit hutch was cut. Indeed, unsuspecting young lads from offices round about might be sent in there for a 'long weight' or even striped paint - the staff were accustomed to such requests! Many goods were priced in code letters, so that customers would not necessarily be aware of the actual cost! This was an old established practice that was discontinued in the fifties.

Two long serving members of staff, Cecil Perry and Fred French had worked there all their lives, apart from Great War service and knew just about all there was to know in the paint, tools and gardening trades. Cecil, who was expert at cutting glass, on a wide table at the rear of the shop, had a dry sense of humour, not always appreciated by customers. When one asked for a length of cord, he would produce a roll from a drawer, but before snipping off the required amount, declare, "Oh, somebody's cut the end off." The reality of this remark was often lost on the customer. Farmers from across Essex were regular customers on Fridays, buying barbed wire, drums of disinfectant or plough traces, while their wives chose cleaning materials or saucepans from the varied stock. Anyone requiring methylated spirits, turpentine, white spirit (also known as 'sub-turps') or linseed oil merely had to take an empty lemonade bottle into the shop, to have it filled from reserve drums kept at the back, while down in the cellar a tank contained hundreds of gallons of paraffin, ready to be drawn up by a hand pump into customers' cans. Down there could also be found galvanised baths, chicken feeders and brooms.

Putty was dispensed by hand from a drum and wrapped in newspaper, while behind the main counter, dozens of wooden drawers held coloured paint powder, scissors, tacks, an assortment of knives and so on. Whitewash was available in powder or liquid form and distemper pre-empted the use of emulsion paint for walls. Tins of Robbialac and other brands of paint were stacked from floor to ceiling and a hand operated key cutting machine stood on a shelf. One did not have to buy pre-packeted nails, as today, but could purchase them by weight; similarly, screws were sold by the dozen - or even less. There was a story, often repeated, about a lady who asked for a quarter of a pound of six-inch nails - and received just three, with a four inch to make up the weight! After Hance's took over an electrical shop next door, anyone being invited to select from stock on the upper two floors, would be conducted through a maze of storerooms lined with shelves holding boxes of screws, sandpaper, electric appliances and paint brushes, before reaching the final winding staircase and a room stacked with rolls of wallpaper.

Through Angel Yard, beside the shop one could visit Drivers, a reliable printers, another well established firm, one of many in old Chelmsford and to complete this side of the ancient street, Thomas Moy's coal office was part of the White Hart building, which had a long covered yard and at the far end, Jack Petchey operated a private car hire business. The Bell Hotel was next, but when it was demolished, the retail market relocated there and in the waste land behind, known as Bell Meadow.

On the opposite side of the street to Hasler & Hance was Leech's, the only gunsmiths in town, patronised regularly by farmers seeking to dispose of rabbits or shoot pheasants and the two businesses eventually became one. They also sold fishing tackle and heavy knives. On this side of the street were Essex Studios, photographers, a Hugh Wright's butcher's, John Duttons, printers and rear entrances to High Street shops.

It was possible to stand in Tindal Square and count no less than seven public houses. The Golden Lion was on the corner of Market Road and Duke Street (demolished to make way for Norwich Union offices) and other pubs included the Bell, White Hart, Spotted Dog, Dolphin, Saracen's Head and Market House. Not many pubs sold food, apart from packets of Smith's crisps, each with a little twist of blue paper containing salt, so you could enjoy them in just two flavours - plain or salted.

Dining areas that admitted children were almost unknown.

Across the pavement outside many pubs were wooden trapdoors, which were opened up when heavy lorries delivered barrels of beer, to be slowly and carefully rolled down to the cellar below, guided by rope and strong hands. Wooden crates of bottled beer and cordials were also part of the delivery - perhaps by green Charrington's lorries, which were steam driven, a fire being visible below, or by black painted lorries of Mann, Crossman and Paulin.

The Spotted Dog

AMATEUR DRAMATICS

Chelmsford has for many years been well-served by amateur theatrical companies and in the days before television came to occupy so many of our leisure hours, this was one of the principal ways, setting aside sport and going to the cinema, in which citizens enjoyed themselves, either as performers or in the audience.

The foremost company, still putting on annual productions, was Chelmsford Amateur Operatic & Dramatic Society, their first show being Gilbert and Sullivan's *HMS Pinafore* in 1920. Their plush programmes in 1938, when *Rose Marie* was presented and again the next year, for *The Belle of New York*, included photographs of producer Madge Macklin, musical director Charles Hambourg, who conducted a twenty strong orchestra and of the president, Councillor Sidney C Taylor, the Mayor.

Some well-known local business people took part in productions over the years, among them, prominent chiropodist Cecil Bocking (who generously gave free treatment to the tired feet of nurses at Chelmsford Hospital). Cast lists also portrayed several familiar names which formed a nucleus of favourites regularly cropping up in concerts and plays by other societies. Artistes such as Peggy Green, Freddy Munnion, Audrey Parrett, Maurice Phillips, Audrey Cutts, Leonard Pease, Gilbert Torry and his brother Alec all lent their talents elsewhere, indeed Gilbert formed his own concert party 'The Torreadors' in the twenties.

But smaller organisations also put on regular shows, among them Chelmsford Play-reading Club, Marconi Social Club Drama Section, St Peter's Players, YMCA Drama Club and Hoffmann Players. In attendance at every show were the quaintly named 'perruquiers', who applied make-up to the cast; the same names, Percy Russell, Reginald Fish and Peggy Green appeared in programmes of a number of societies.

Oldest established of the societies was St Peter's Players, whose very first production was *Tilly of Bloomsbury* in 1926, and they continued to present a play every year, in the Cathedral Hall, until 1939: Percy Russell was their producer. On several occasions, the Players took their annual production to the leper home at East Hanningfield, where there was a hall with a small stage and they played to a most appreciative audience. Augmented by members of the congregation and choir, they also put on Nativity Plays in the church and when Canon Barrow was Vicar, he directed them. Many rehearsals were held in Toc H hall, next to the church.

In 1931, Essex branches of the Mothers' Union produced a full-length version of John Bunyan's *Pilgrim's Progress* in the Cathedral Hall. My mother, Violet, took the part of Apollyon - The Devil - who threatened Christian, the leading character, with the words, "Prepare thyself to die, for here will I spill thy soul". There followed a sword fight, in which Christian triumphed over evil. My mother's red lined black cloak, horned headdress and wooden sword - all home made - are still cherished by the family.

Quite a few groups organised concerts, a relatively easy way to raise funds, providing they could call on their own dancers, conjuror, singers, comedian and instrumentalist. Chelmsford Hockey Club's concert in 1938 is an example of this strategy. Non-members Douglas Adams (Stanley Holloway's monologues), Peggy Green and Freddy Munnion (humour at the piano), Jean Mossman (impressionist) and Percy Russell's company in a series of sketches provided most of the entertainment.

Footlights were installed along the front of the stage at almost every production, consisting of a row of black metal boxes, each containing a powerful reflector lamp, with a coloured gel across the top, beneath a wire protection grid. Overhead lighting units were intended to be inconspicuous, hidden amongst the 'flies', lines of drapes from one side of the stage to the other - a far cry from the row on row of spot and flood lights so visible in every theatre today.

Upon the arrival of 'crooning', people who had previously been accustomed to traditional English songs, by contraltos, tenors or baritones, were now more than a little startled to see a young man wailing a love song close up to a microphone, perhaps imitating the style of Bing Crosby and some felt this was an intrusion into their rather staid ideas of what a concert turn should be like. But of course, younger members of the audiences thought the modern music scene was fantastic. Nothing has changed!

Girl Guides, Boy Scouts, churches, schools and the factories, all contributed to the wealth of leisure pursuits and entertainment available, though there was a saying in pre-war Chelmsford that there was 'nothing to do', a situation easily denied by a glance in the columns of the local press, showing reports of a whole miscellany of town activities.

In London, Lupino Lane was appearing in *Me and My Girl*, in which a dance was seen for the first time - the Lambeth Walk. It was a bit of fun (especially shouting the 'Oi'), easy to learn and, like another novelty dance which became prominent about the same time, the Palais Glide, very soon became popular, particularly amongst people who were not confident with conventional fox-trots, quick-steps and so on. Dances were held at the Corn Exchange, Odeon and elsewhere every week.

As well as organisations for young people, there were dancing schools, among them Doris Rodd's, which practised in a studio in Crane Court, beside Spaldings and the larger Maidie Russell school. Maidie was well known for the excellent quality of her shows, including pantomimes, which she presented with very talented young performers for a number of years.

Although most programmes stated both Christian and surname of players, some Victorian practices, when artists were referred to as 'Mr' or 'Miss', still lingered. The 1933 cast of a play at All Saints Church, Boarded Barns, were simply referred to as 'Mrs Butcher, Mrs Roast, Mrs Gifford' and so on. Many people never got around to using Christian names, even when they had known each other for years.

HIGH STREET, SMITHY AND FORTY THIEVES

Next to Cramphorn's main shop and Head Office was the Scotch Wool Stores, then Martin's provisions and Co-op drapers, which one day suffered a disastrous fire. Further along was yet another grocers, Peark's. Joy's was a popular ladies' wear shop, beside Fletcher's, a butcher and Thomas Danels, watchmaker. The office of the *Essex Weekly News* and their printing works adjoined J G Bond's, which had a very long frontage and arcade of display windows. On one upper floor was a restaurant, much used by ladies having a gossip over morning coffee or afternoon tea and there was also a photographic studio, where many sat for their portraits. The store, now Debenham's, was once, besides the familiar drapers, ladies' and gents' outfitters and travel bureau, also funeral furnishers, as was Bolingbroke's, opposite.

When Halford's cycle shop across the road was having a new fascia installed, it was noticed that painted on the old one underneath was 'J G Bond', though I have never seen any history of old Chelmsford recording Bond's being on that side of the street. Perhaps the sign had been recycled.

Adjacent to Bond's, before Marks and Spencer took over the property, were Hick's café and a cleaners, an entrance to a yard being either side. Easiphit Shoes and Lavell's (previously Meeson's) confectioners came next to Fitch sports outfitters, which changed over to Boons bakers. At Macfisheries, the assistants worked throughout the year in the open. There was no frontage, shoppers simply stepped off the pavement directly between sloping counters laden with crabs, shrimps, scallops, many varieties of fish and copious lumps of ice. The red tiled floor was often hosed down, the shop always kept clean and fresh.

In front of this and Boot's Chemists, the last shop before Springfield Road, was a bus stop. For several years a man with a sign hung round his neck announcing he was disabled in the Great War stood here every weekday, offering boxes of matches for sale from a little tray. Other men regularly seen in town were road-sweepers, who pushed three-wheeled khaki painted wooden carts, as they went about their task, collecting rubbish from pavements and gutters.

The white stone Conduit commanded the middle of High Street at Springfield Road corner, where three way traffic was controlled by a policeman, who during inclement weather would hang his black uniform cape on a hook inside the structure. But when traffic lights were first introduced, here and elsewhere, there was no amber, just red and green. Incredibly, they changed simultaneously, with no pause and cars would try to halt at red, as other traffic crossing over moved off at green, at the same time!

On the corner, Fifty Shilling Tailors sold men's suits - for exactly that price - and was next to Woolworth's. Above the windows of this American owned store, in gold embossed lettering on red background, was a legend which disappeared many years ago – '2D, 3D & 6D STORE   F W WOOLWORTH & CO.'. It was possible to buy no end of household items, crockery, toys, tools, films and gramophone records for no more than six old pence! So for a small outlay, a complete matching tea service in an attractive pattern could be purchased, a piece at a time.

It was customary to leave a bicycle leaning against the kerb outside a shop, safe in the knowledge that it would still be there, after one had finished shopping - padlocks were not a necessity. A friend once left his bike outside Woolworth's, then met some pals and walked home to Rainsford End with them. On realising his mistake, he walked back, to find it was still safely in the same place!

Lipton's, next door, was one of a chain of grocer's shops, formerly owned by Scotsman Sir Thomas Lipton, who also imported tea and coffee from his own plantations in Ceylon. His hobby was racing yachts and he competed in the Americas Cup several times, until 1930. His shops were eventually sold to the Allied Group, which also owned Maypole and Home & Colonial.

Banham butchers, a dress shop, Norman Stanley wireless dealer and a shoe shop were also here and, for a while, an off-licence. Finally, before the Stone Bridge, was Nelson Murdoch piano showroom and an imposing, red brick Methodist Church, which was eventually demolished in favour of Cater's supermarket.

The other side of the bridge is the start of Moulsham Street and the first ever neon sign seen in town depicted, in glowing red, Body's the chemists. A Hawke's sweetshop adjoined it, then Rankin's drapers' arcade of windows, displaying dressed models and decoratively arranged lengths of materials. One of their employees was Billy Jones, a very short man who rode a heavy bicycle fitted with a carrier frame at the front and was well known for whistling loudly, calling out friendly greetings as he went about the town, delivering parcels from the shop.

The Regent Theatre came next, a cinema with a long history of music hall, which was used every year for productions by Chelmsford Amateur Operatic and Dramatic Society and still retained its cramped dressing rooms and heavy stage curtains, operated by turning a handle. The Society used arc lamps to provide spot and floodlights, operated from the balcony and they smoked when first switched on.

Beside the theatre was Stapleton's, formerly Archer's, pork butchers, then came Turner's basket shop, a really olde worlde establishment, where handmade baskets of all types festooned the doorway and frontage. One had to climb stone steps to the entrance door, to inspect the many shopping and pet baskets displayed across the floor and suspended from the ceiling, in the gloomy and rather mysterious interior. One had the feeling, on entering, that time had stopped there in the days of Charles Dickens.

An open fronted greengrocers, Harris's was on the corner, its counters extending round into Baddow Road and in the space of the next few yards there was a small Eastern National booking office, which at one time served as a booking office for Pickfords Removals, a covered bus shelter and public convenience. A sweets and cigarette kiosk came before a yard leading to the stage door and back entrance of the Regent cinema, where we sometimes queued for the cheaper seats.

Right next to the yard, under a rough roof, a blacksmith could once be seen wielding his hammer over an anvil, while a horse stood by the blazing fire and blackened bellows, waiting to be shod. The smithy was replaced by a barber's in the early thirties, but not before that ancient scene had been imprinted on my memory.

Mrs Rison's sweetshop came next, beside Laurie Levett's greengrocery. He was the brother of District Nurse, Nellie Levett, and also had a 'round', calling weekly on customers with a van loaded with fruit and vegetables. Mann's, which adjoined, sold leather for boot mending - many people owned a solid iron shoe last and repaired the family's shoes at home. Before the arrival of the Ritz cinema, there was an entrance here to King's Head Meadow.

So, back to Tindal Square, where stood Judge Tindal's statue. Behind him were The Market House, a popular little pub with a 'snug', run by landlord Cecil Judge and, next door, National Provincial Bank. Adjoining that was Midland Bank and an alleyway separated them from the *Essex Chronicle* offices and works, where the thunder of printing machinery was a familiar sound every Thursday, producing next day's edition. The paper was first established in 1764 and proprietor, Mr J Ockleford Thompson, when mayor, was killed when a lone German plane dropped a bomb on his house in London Road in 1940. He had previously been mayor from 1928 to 1930 and in 1938.

Always fascinated by printing, I enjoyed using a John Bull outfit, consisting of a set of rubber letters, which were inserted in a wooden holder and pressed on an ink pad, to produce a rather crude line of print, so was especially pleased to be invited to the *Essex Chronicle* compositor room, where typesetting by hot metal linotype operators took place, as they sat before a line of machines, making pages for the Friday paper.

Senior reporters were J C Chaplin and F J Tapp, but a former Grammar School pupil, Gilbert Saunders, who joined the team, earned the nickname of 'Scoop', following some outstanding reporting stories. His inventive tale of a ghost at a Great Leighs pub kept readers intrigued for weeks.

Along this side of High Street was a leading estate agent, Alfred Darby, where Frank Burrell and Albert Caton were prominent auctioneers. Early Bunn, a chemist and Cleale's ironmongers later changed to furriers Saks & Brendlor and Christy's lighting showroom, beside International Stores. Between that and another countrywide grocers, Sainsbury's, which had opened in 1922, was a walkway through to Tindal Street and then came the shop of John Dutton, stationers, who also had a printing works on the premises. On entering Sainsbury's, a delicious and distinctive smell of fresh produce met one - a mixture of bacon, cheese, butter and ham. On each side of an immaculate white tiled floor, decorated with black mosaic patterns, was a long counter, from front to back of the store, high wooden stools standing at intervals for use by weary shoppers. All Sainsbury's stores were basically identical in design, both in frontage and interior layout. The founder, John James Sainsbury, who opened his first shop in 1869 (and died in 1928), one day noticed a little boy breathing on a display of bacon and put in a protective glass screen for the front of all counters. Hygiene was of paramount importance and counter hands worked diligently to keep their section spotless. After closing, marble counters, tiled walls and floor were scrubbed, brass weights and scales were polished and, once a week, rails used to display sides of bacon were taken down and burnished.

Children visiting the store were intrigued by two activities - first, the little cups into which customers' money was placed and, after a tug on a handle, sped down the shop on an overhead wire to the cash desk, which was right across the far end, then came speeding back with the change. Secondly, at a black marble counter, after a particular variety of butter had been selected from the big blocks on display, it was seen to be cut through with a wooden knife, weighed and patted into an oblong shape, the 'butterman' using two wooden 'pats'. One of them had an embossed pattern, which became transferred to the butter before it was wrapped in greaseproof paper, having been weighed on elaborate pink and white scales. Those salesmen were swift and very skilled - always seeming to cut off the exact amount of butter required - though, of course, they were doing that job all day!

There was a minimum of three kinds of margarine and four of butter (at about a shilling a pound) and eggs were displayed in baskets on a bed of hay. Pheasants, partridge, grouse, chickens, hares and rabbits were for sale in season, together with suggested recipes and a selection of cooked meats, including beef and sausages, was there to entice hungry customers. Prime cooked York ham was a speciality, displayed on pink and white china stands.

Twenty types of English and foreign cheeses were on show, Cheddar being the most popular. Fresh beef might be Scotch or from Argentina (which was cheaper) and Canterbury lamb came from New Zealand. A bacon-slicing machine (another fascinating activity to watch) could be adjusted to produce any number of thicknesses, according to customers' choice. Finally, own brand groceries available included tea, cocoa, pickle, custard, fruit juice and tinned fruit.

Smiths, the drapers, a very pleasant store, was well known for having an extensive selection of fabrics and haberdashery. When asked the price of a particular material, an assistant might answer, "One and eleven three," indicating one shilling and eleven pence three farthings per yard (just under 10p). Sometimes when paying for goods and there was a fraction of a penny due in change, a blue paper packet of pins was given in lieu.

Next shop along was Lennard's shoes, then Woodward's and Fuller's, both selling men's wear, Norwich Union Fire Insurance office, Crafts Shoes and Freke's confectioners (which became Peachey's). A public convenience, partly concealed behind green trellis, was situated here, almost on the corner of New London Road, but it was somewhat conspicuous on Friday market days, because there would inevitably be a long queue of patient ladies waiting to use the facilities! An entrance for males was round the corner in Tindal Street.

On the other side of London Road, J H Clarke's, where typewriters could be purchased for £3 in 1938, was perhaps the leading stationers in town. Lloyd's Bank and Clarke's occupied an island and the narrow tail end of Tindal Street separated them from F Luckin Smith's grocery, which was eventually sold to Budgen's.

Two respected local businesses, Bolingbroke's, drapers and costumiers, established in 1876 and Wenley's, house furnishers, which began in Baddow Road in 1845 and moved to High Street in 1898, occupied the next two shops, the latter having an extensive glass windowed arcade, leading through to London Road. In either showroom, one might be served by a member of the respective family - like Alderman Stanley Bolingbroke, or

Robert Wenley, who had joined the company aged eighteen. Wenley's also offered removals and carpet cleaning. An upholstery apprentice there in 1937 was paid five shillings a week and the same amount was earned by a shop assistant at Bolingbroke's, rising to seven shillings and sixpence, after a year's employment.

Montague Burton, Rego clothiers and Hepworth's, all tailors, were side by side here, before H H Cass, a well stocked cycle and wireless shop, locally owned. Gosling's shoes and Halford's cycle shop came next to another F Luckin Smith store, though this one sold domestic hardware, not groceries. It had a large staff and offered a wide variety of chinaware and kitchen utensils. Next door was Singer Sewing Machines, then Johnson's cleaners and a butcher, Dewhirst's. Curry's, who then dealt in bicycles, took over premises that were formerly a sweetshop.

The Queen's Head, an ancient and much used public house, which can be seen in many old photos and prints of the High Street, occupied a position opposite Springfield Road. It was next to Osborne's tobacconist, then came Maypole Dairy and Oram's jewellers, later taken over by Webber's, whose main shop was in Duke Street.

Between the pub and Stone Bridge were several small shops, including Greens opticians, owned by Mr Cutts and men's outfitters Fox, which offered Grammar School regulation uniforms, including suits, priced at no more than forty five shillings, ties for half-a-crown and school caps at three and sixpence. Owner Mr Fox was an alderman of the borough. There were also Home & Colonial grocery store and, next door, a butchers, before it became Kays, a cut price grocers. E L Hunt, builders' merchants, displaying bathroom ware in the windows, Jeffrey's tailors and Williams, a ladies' dress shop, completed the range of high street stores.

Across the bridge, in Moulsham, Fosters, which catered for inexpensive men's and boys' clothing, Phillips shoes, International Stores, Plattin's chemists (formerly Warren's) and the Co-operative Furniture store and registered office occupied the buildings as far as Barrack Square, a narrow cul-de-sac. At the Co-op office, dividend that had accrued on customers' purchases was paid out every year to members taking along their black passbook, in which a record was kept. On the opposite corner to the Co-op was Bond's Furniture showroom, where, every year, a miniature 'Ideal Home Exhibition' was held - very intriguing for youngsters walking through the layout of rooms, perhaps imagining themselves at the real thing - at Olympia.

HOUSE CALLS AND SYRUP OF FIGS

When the milkman arrived on his round, driving a horse drawn cart, with a high wheel on either side, he would fill a brass bound milk carrier from the big, shiny churn fixed at the front (in the summer, the churn was enveloped in a white cover, to protect it from the sun). On the side of the carrier hung half-pint and one pint measures and he would dip one of these into the milk, then pour it into a jug held by his customer, waiting at the door. Returning to the cream painted cart, he stepped on the back and the shafts would rise at the horse's sides, amid a jangling of brasses on the black leather harness. Boys sometimes cadged a ride beside him, for a few yards, as he again took the reins. When milk was, in due course, delivered in bottles, it was supplied in not only pints, but also quarts and half pints, as required and the milkman came every day, including Sunday.

Our regular order for the baker was a large white and a small brown loaf - the latter being available in brands unknown today - Daren or Vitbe. A linen coupon was attached underneath Vitbe and these were collected for free gifts. When the baker had handed over the usual two loaves from his ample wicker basket at the back door, he would request just, "Fourpence three farthings, if you please."

A coalman came every few months, emptying hundredweight sacks of coal into our solid wood, homemade bunker. "Make sure you count ten," warned my mother, just in case the man was dishonest and left us one bag short! But he always brought the right number. One of our infrequent, but most essential visitors was talkative Mr Goldsmith, a chimney sweep, who lived in King's Road and kept our dining room chimney free from soot.

Mr Charlie Chaplin of Galleywood, arrived in the road just two days a year, driving his horse and cart, which had no sides and was heaped with fresh green home-grown peas. At the back was a cylindrical wooden measure and Mr Chaplin, who wore a bowler hat, would announce his presence with the cry, "Peas, tuppence a peck", generously over-filling the measure with peas when a customer approached.

Another, more regular trader, commonly known as 'Fishy', toured the estates around town in the evenings in a high black van and when he stopped at the usual spots, would open a flap on one side to form a counter. Several people who had been attracted by the customary 'honk-honk' of the motor horn were already waiting, to buy their penn'orth of chips and piece of fish. Frying was achieved by heat from an enclosed fire, black smoke rising from a chimney in the roof and a fishy smell lingered long after the van had moved off to the next stop.

A Walls ice cream vendor, on his tricycle, was a welcome summer visitor and the little man who came to our area would park his trike at the wide entrance to Admirals Park, before coming up Park Avenue to Warwick Square, constantly ringing the bell on his handlebars, to announce his arrival. On the front of his navy blue cold compartment, below a 'STOP ME AND BUY ONE' sign, was an enamelled price list, offering a selection including large bricks at 1/6d, threepenny choc bars, wafers for twopence and, cheapest of all, Snofrutes for a penny. These can best be described as triangular blocks of flavoured ice, wrapped in blue cardboard. The man might cut one in half, for a ha'penny, if you asked politely!

A man riding a tricycle and offering similar ices, under the name 'Eldorado', which some people thought were creamier than Walls, appeared on the streets for a year or so, but he disappeared. Perhaps the powerful Walls organisation bought out this competitor.

Along Rainsford Road, not far from Maltese Road, was Wright's, a not very smart confectioner's shop, with red curtains and an orange lampshade in the window, where we could take a pudding basin and have it filled with home made ice cream, though it had a custard flavour! Stedman's ladies' hairdressers adjoined it on one side and Thompson's shoe repairers on the other.

The Corona man called once a week, with a tasty selection of cordials and fizzy drinks. My favourite was cherryade, but some of my friends enjoyed other brands, like Tizer and R White's American Cream Soda. A drink we made at home was Eiffel Tower, lemonade crystals to which water was added. Sold in a small, square sided bottle, the crystals could be eaten, but they were a bit sharp, just like lemons.

As father had 'signed the pledge' when a lad, in the 1880's, we never had intoxicating liquor in the house. Even at Christmas, the strongest drink we had was Stone's Ginger Wine. So we never entered a pub, though occasionally went to the Jug & Bottle at the Black Bull in Rainsford Road, to buy Macpherson's ginger beer.

"Any old rags?" was a cry we occasionally heard from a 'rag and bone' man, trundling up the street with a horse and dilapidated cart, piled high with old brass bedsteads, heaps of cast off clothing and the odd pram or discarded kettle - forerunner of the recycling amenities we are accustomed to today. When a child approached with some unwanted items from home, the reward might be a goldfish in a jar, or a balloon. But if any money was offered, it was a case of "Is that all he gave you? The old rogue!" from mother. Gypsies, selling their home made clothes pegs, or bunches of primroses also knocked on the door regularly every year.

A profusion of houseflies in the home was quite common and our usual method of slaughter was with a rolled up newspaper - we did not favour sticky flypapers. One year, my mother gave me a penny for every twenty killed! A more scientific method of getting rid of them was by spraying with Flit. A Flit spray consisted of a white metal cylinder with a handle, rather similar to a bicycle pump, with a nozzle at one end, fixed to a refillable container, needing a pump action to release a spray of fly-killer. The invention of aerosols to do the job was way in the future and old-timers can still be heard to exclaim, "Flit that fly," when one is in the room. Simple and effective wasp traps were made by covering the top of a jam jar with paper, with a hole in the middle and water and honey to tempt them inside.

My brother enjoyed building working models with a Meccano set and I had 'Tinkertoy', a wooden construction kit, but we both loved to visit a very fortunate friend who had a Hornby train layout in his 'playroom'. Underneath most of our metal clockwork toys, like cars and tractors, was printed the country of origin and if it simply said DRGM, we knew that meant it was made in Germany. In the early thirties, with the disastrous Great War still prominent in many minds, we used to interpret those initials as 'Dirty Rotten German Make'. Another toy often played with was a wooden fort, complete with a drawbridge and lead soldiers in red Guards uniform and black busby (bought at Woolworth's for tuppence each). How often those heads broke off at the fragile neck and were fixed back on with a matchstick pushed into the hollow body! Many toys had components made of celluloid, which, although very colourful was highly inflammable and if it should catch fire gave off black acrid smoke.

We also played a variety of card games with special packs, like Lexicon, Pit, Sorry! and Cathedrals and often built five storey 'houses' with three or four packs of standard playing cards, deftly removing the lower cards, one by one, until the house finally collapsed. My father taught us cribbage, his favourite indoor game, but when we acquired a table tennis set, everyone wanted to play, which entailed first clearing much of the dining room, to give us sufficient space. A most hilarious game we had, which I have never seen anywhere else was Wibbley Wobb, where a small goal was fixed each end of the table and a wooden puck needed to be dribbled through, by each opposing player, with the aid of a pusher consisting of a triangular 'foot' connected to a handle by fourteen inches of flexible wire. The frustration at being unable to control that foot and hilarity it caused can only be imagined, but we did manage to score goals.

One family member completed the new Vernon's football pool coupon every week, with a very rare small win and on Saturday evening we all had to remain quiet while he sat by the radio checking the match results.

When my little 'gang' of boys were on our bikes, we would often imagine ourselves tearing around the car racing circuit of Brooklands, in Surrey. Sometimes we cycled the three miles to Galleywood, where, close to the racecourse, was what we called The Wall of Death (after the motor cycle side-show of that name in fairgrounds). It was a track in a little valley among the gorse bushes and if you pedalled hard, it was possible to ride down one side and rise to the top on the other. Not all the boys dared to try it. My parents bought me a new bike after I had passed the scholarship, a black 'racing' style, with dropped handlebars, narrow wheels and Sturmey Archer gears, which was the 'in-thing' style at the time. It cost five pounds.

Two stands still survived from the days when Galleywood racecourse surrounded the parish church. The white and green larger one, eventually taken over by Marconi's, was boarded up and inaccessible, but the other of simple wooden steps was ideal to play on and under. There was also, at one time, a rostrum that the race starter used to mount.

We also liked to cycle to Pleshey Mount, or to pick bluebells for our mothers at 'Baddow Rodney', as it was known. In our early teens, we ventured on bikes as far as Maldon, twelve miles away and played in the park open-air swimming pool. Traffic was very light, compared with today's busy roads.

A few doors away from our Park Avenue home, lived Jack Steele, who, like his father and brother Harold in Baddow Road, by the Isolation Hospital, was a builder. Very obliging Jack was much in demand locally, especially to householders needing someone to climb up long ladders to sort out roof problems, or provide all the materials for a home made concrete pathway. Other nearby residents included very precise, 'vertically challenged' Mr Percy Burdon, who walked to his office in County Hall, every day, habitually wearing a bowler hat; and flame-haired Mrs Morgan, who ran a private school in her home, with never more than half a dozen pupils, all with severe learning difficulty. She had a son, Michael, whom we boys were told not to play with (we never did find out why), so of course we liked to chat with him whenever possible!

Our house had not been wired for electrical appliances, so there were no sockets anywhere. Nobody had a 'fridge or washing machine, the only common appliance being an iron. When my mother used it, it was plugged into a two-way adapter beneath the lampshade in the centre of the living room. As she ironed, the bead decorated shade swung alarmingly back and forth - the simple twin flex from the ceiling rose coping with such dangerous treatment for several years. Above the lampshade, a rise and fall mechanism which enabled the light to be pulled down nearer to the dining table beneath, when my father was writing letters, included pulleys and a ceramic counterweight containing hundreds of steel balls.

Mother would sit for hours at her Singer treadle sewing machine by the dining room window making garments for herself, relatives or friends, or mending linen household items, while above her was our pet bird in a cage, singing in accompaniment to the regular throb of the machine. Canaries were then the most popular birds; the era of budgerigars had not arrived.

All floors were covered in linoleum, with a rug by the fireplace - wall-to-wall carpeting was years ahead. The weekly wash was accomplished with the aid of a corrugated washboard, in a galvanised bath of water, which had been heated on the gas cooker. The kitchen table, on which the bath stood when in use, was covered in 'American cloth', a waterproof material available in a variety of colourful patterns on a white background and bought by the yard from a draper's or market stall. On Friday night - bath night, when we always used red Lifebuoy soap, that galvanised bath, half full of hot water was carried upstairs, to be tipped into the bath, where only cold water was piped in. Thankfully, in 1933, we had a Ewart water heater installed, emitting a very loud 'pop' when a pilot light ignited the gas, triggered by turning on a hot tap. We also had a new bathroom built, to include a toilet, which until then, had been outside.

Friday night was also memorable as when I had a weekly dose of syrup of figs!

'HEIL' AT THE SPORTS, CARNIVALS & BRYN JONES

The three main factories all had their own sports fields, Hoffmann's being in Rainsford Road, while Crompton's was situated just off the lower end of Wood Street and Marconi's was in Beehive Lane. Sports days, especially Inter Works - between the three factories - were eagerly anticipated every year, with full programmes of running, hurdling, cycling and other field events. Most exciting of all were 'Devil take the hindmost' cycle races, in which the last competitor would be eliminated at each lap. There were often spills, when St John's Ambulance crews would go into action. The tug-of-war, between the heftiest men from each factory, was always a well-supported event, accompanied by loud cheers from spectators.

An impressive array of prizes on display included not only cups, shields and plaques, but a dazzling selection of cut glass vases, biscuit barrels and rose bowls, plus canteens of cutlery and other luxury household items, all generously donated by directors of the three companies involved.

One feature of the Hoffmann field was a quoits arena, where participants threw heavy horseshoes, to try and land them around a low post set into a flat clay bed. A horse was also kept there, for pulling the grass cutter and heavy roller. We lived not far away and my father was able to take his wheelbarrow to the field occasionally, to secure a load of manure for the garden.

One year, when Essex schools participated in a joint sports day there, the organisers had decided on a very controversial gesture. During a march past by all the competitors, they were required to raise their left arms in a *heil* salute. The Nazis had not long risen to power in Germany and, although it was not the same, right arm *heil*, it did not meet with everyone's approval.

Another popular annual event in which employees of the three big factories participated, was the annual Hospital Carnival, organised by Mr R G Morrish, secretary of the Chelmsford and Essex Hospital in London Road. This was then the town's only hospital, as St Johns in Wood Street was an infirmary, mostly for the elderly and sometimes known by the Victorian designation as The Workhouse. Broomfield hospital was devoted only to the care of TB patients, who had individual wards opening on to a balcony and were exposed to the open air for much of the time, as part of their treatment.

The carnival was a major event in the town calendar. Floats, bands and walking entrants were marshalled in Rectory Lane and preceded along Broomfield Road, Duke Street and through the town, the mayor taking the salute from the steps of the Shire Hall. Just occasionally, an exhibit, such as a sailing boat with a high mast, was found to be too tall to negotiate Duke Street railway bridge and, after causing much confusion, was turned round and re-routed back to Rectory Lane and through the higher New Street bridge.

From High Street and then Moulsham Street, the procession turned right through Writtle Road and down London Road, back into High Street, Market Road and the recreation ground, where it dispersed. Traditionally, people on the three factory floats then wrecked each other's displays!

A rule that 'no water or missiles' should be thrown from floats, was largely ignored, for flour bombs and water sprays often showered on the thousands of onlookers, who mostly took it all in good part, clapping and cheering the Carnival Queen and others as they passed. Hospital nurses were always applauded, eight of them carrying a large bed sheet, in which we were encouraged to aim our pennies. The Boys' Brigade Band unfortunately had a reputation of being out of tune, but it all added to the fun, while an Essex Regiment band and Grammar School Corps of Drums were usually there to provide marching music. Smart troops of Boy Scouts and Girl Guides always took part, the latter being led, for many years, by Mrs G Harknett.

For a shilling, a solid metal carnival 'immunity' badge could be bought during the week, which was supposed to exempt you from contributing to tins being rattled by the many collectors on the procession route, though half the fun of watching was to successfully aim a penny and land it firmly on a passing float.

The procession was headed, every year, by John Fewell, dressed as John Bull, riding an immaculate horse - and fire engines were always last to pass by. Tom Crees was the well-known Chief Marshal for many years and when he retired in 1965, I had the pleasure of succeeding him.

One entrance to The Rec. was from Viaduct Road and on carnival day, trestle tables were placed across the pathway, beneath a high railway arch, where stewards sold entrance tickets. Similar barriers were set up at the other entrances to the park.

Local organisations had their own sideshows in the Rec., which it was hoped people would patronise before spending all their money in the visiting fair. This was sited in the park on an area behind houses in Park Road, huge, noisy steam engines providing electrical power for dodgems, roundabouts and thousands of lights. One of the rides was the Caterpillar, an undulating roundabout where, soon after it started, a green canvas hood moved over the heads of car occupants, leaving some of them squealing in the dark, but giving couples an opportunity for a few kisses, before the hood rolled back at the end! It was extremely tame by today's standards, but a bit of excitement then. Tallest structure on the fairground was a helter-skelter, while the wide swinging chair-o-plane roundabout was about the scariest ride of all.

Contributing to afternoon displays in the park arena, the fire brigade also caused amusement. Some years, they played 'football', propelling a large coloured ball into goals by squirting water from their hoses, occasionally spraying the good natured crowds. At other times, their displays were unintentionally humorous, when they 'rescued' someone from a replica house that was supposed to blaze, but only managed a short red flare, before it extinguished itself. How we cheered!

There was more cheering and laughter in the years when a Greasy Pole competition was organised. A well greased pole was erected across the river and two teams of lads would take turns to attempt to knock an opponent off, by hitting out with pillows and the spectators could not conceal their glee when either or both of them fell in the water.

A grand fireworks display at the end of the day, was made even more spectacular by taking place across the river and reflecting in the water, to loud choruses of 'aaah' from tired onlookers, who had cheered the long procession, thrown their pennies on to floats, watched the prize giving and enjoyed fairground rides.

Next day, Sunday, festivities were brought to a close with a 'drumhead service' on the Essex County Cricket ground, Essex Regiment drums, covered by Union Flags, acting as an altar. There had been other activities during the week, including a 'mile of pennies', when coins could be placed on the kerbside for a mile through the town, to support hospital funds. In some years a procession of illuminated boats was organised to take place on one evening and they made a glorious sight as they glided by crowds gathered at dusk near the river in the Rec.

On Wednesday there had been a Tiny Tots Parade, starting from King Edward Avenue, for children not old enough to take part in the main carnival. Grammar School boys had Wednesday afternoons off and one or two were called upon to act as marshals for the little procession, with Mr Morrish himself at the head to guide the children.

Located near the Park Road entrance used to be three trophies from the Great War - two grey field guns, with little wheels that could be easily manipulated to 'direct fire' were marvellous for boys to play on, but a military tank, which had stood nearby, was removed in the mid thirties. A café and bowling green, surrounded by well-maintained flowerbeds were also in this area.

At the other side of the park, Territorials constructed a Bailey bridge across the river, facilitating access to the football stadium in New Writtle Street. When the most famous team of the time, Arsenal, came to play Chelmsford City in an FA Cup match, the days of their star footballer, Alex James, famous for his long baggy white shorts, were long gone, but they brought their new player, the 'most expensive signing ever', Bryn Jones. He had cost Arsenal the then record sum of fourteen thousand pounds!

"Up the City, wheel 'em in", was the cry from local fans, but unfortunately it didn't help them to beat the Gunners.

HOME SCHOOL FIREWORKS TO WATERHOUSE LANE

We lived opposite one of the playing fields of the Essex Home School for Boys, also known as Essex Industrial School or, as we were warned when young, the place where naughty boys were sent. The boys would often be marshalled past our house, dressed in their drab uniform of grey pullover, shorts and long socks, on an exercising walk through Admirals Park, across fields and back via Roxwell Road. They were not allowed to talk loudly while on their route and there was never any unruly behaviour, which would have been severely dealt with.

One of their teachers, Mr Tucker, lived near us and every 5th November, he would give us fireworks that had been sent to boys by their families and been confiscated. (One never-to-be-forgotten year, my brother went to look in the box while still holding a lighted sparkler and the whole lot ignited, rockets and bangers shooting in all directions!) However, the school did organise a fireworks display for the pupils. Another teacher, a jolly man named Tom Parfitt, was a popular singer, who took part in local concerts and his repertoire, sung in a high tenor voice, always included Christopher Robin.

Every summer the boys were taken on a camping holiday and the son of headmaster Reginald Fish sometimes invited my brother and me to play in the school. How our voices echoed in those high, empty corridors, as we raced through them on the way to the gymnasium and deserted swimming pool, though we didn't enter the water.

Mr Tucker had a son, Vic, who, with his friend Harold Tomalin, living a few doors away, became the town's first 'speed cops'. Both tall, amiable policemen, who remained firm friends until the death of Vic in his seventies, they often parked the powerful police motorbikes outside their homes. Local boys were impressed by the number of dead flies covering the large headlamps, indicating, they felt sure, the furious speed at which the bikes were driven!

Staff frowned on chatting to Home School boys over the railings, which I did occasionally, though perhaps they were afraid boys might be offered cigarettes. My father was the only smoker in our family, he had a rack of pipes, which included a particular favourite he regularly filled with tobacco and puffed away at, filling the room with a pleasant aroma. He also smoked Craven A cigarettes, supplied in a red packet with a black cat logo, usually purchased, priced sixpence for ten, or twenty for a shilling, at a shop owned by Mrs. Williams, at the top of Rainsford Lane, in between Webb's tailors and Chelmsford Tyre Services.

Some cigarettes, so popular then, such as Park Drive (green & red packet), Wills Gold Flake, in yellow packets and Players Navy Cut, with sailor logo, are no longer seen. Our neighbour favoured Ardath, which he bought in pale blue tins of 100, while other people preferred Weights, or Woodbines, both being available in packets of five.

Familiar newspapers too, have disappeared. My mother read the *Daily Sketch*, father the *News Chronicle* and a friend the *Daily Herald*, while on Saturday, the yellow fronted *Weekly Telegraph* magazine was delivered, which we later swapped with next door's green covered *Tit-Bits* and pink *Pearson's Weekly*. On Sundays, we had broadsheet *Reynolds*

News and the sister paper of *Daily Sketch*, the tabloid *Sunday Graphic*. Another popular paper was The *Sunday Dispatch*. Occasionally, we bought *Hulton's Picture Post*, packed full of remarkable black and white photographs, *Everybody's*, which had a lot of red print, *John Bull's Weekly*, full of puzzles, or *Illustrated*, which included colour pictures. Not one of these publications now exists.

Every summer, the *News Chronicle* published photographs of a man they called Lobby Lud, who they said would be in a certain seaside resort that day. If readers spotted him, they could declare, "You are Lobby Lud. I claim the *News Chronicle* prize." They also had to be carrying a copy of that day's paper, to verify they were readers. It all helped to sell more *Chronicles*!

An advertisement regularly appearing in papers and magazines depicted a very muscular 'Charles Atlas' carrying the world on his shoulders, above the slogan, "You too can have a body like mine - in six easy lessons". Below this was a drawing of a puny man and details of how to achieve this magnificent physique - send money for a bodybuilding course. Sunday papers published half a page of advertisements in little squares, including one that offered a drum set, with a base drum, side drum and cymbal, all for ten shillings and sixpence. There was no indication of its size.

A favourite weekly mag. was *Hotspur*, in which could be eagerly followed author Frank Richard's stories of Greyfriars School, with the exploits of Harry Wharton ("I say, you chaps") and chums, including Billy Bunter ("Eeek!"). *The Wizard* and *Magnet* were close second choice. An advert frequently seen in them, beside all the tempting offers of foreign postage stamps 'on approval' was for a Seebackroscope, which was said could be held to the eye, to see who was behind, though why you would ever need one is a mystery. My mother regularly read a woman's magazine, still on sale today, but would be horrified to see the modern editions, with pages devoted to sexual problems.

A magazine that was never seen at home, but secretly read with friends, who had had the courage to buy or even borrow a copy, was *Health and Efficiency*, which included carefully blurred sepia photographs of lithe ladies who were *'au naturel'*. Not a bit like some explicit publications now available, but very daring in those years.

Just as the *Daily Mail* printed exploits every day of Teddy Tail and the *Express* had Rupert Bear, both newspapers sending badges to children joining their club, so the *Sketch* published their children's cartoon, of Japhet. Children joining his Club received a black and yellow badge, to denote that they were an 'Arkub'. Badges were available on joining almost any club - there was the *Sunday Referee*'s Shirley Temple League, Bourneville Cocoa's Cococubs, the League of Ovaltiney's and *Reynolds News*' Sunshine Circle. Chelmsford City football supporters were able to purchase a badge bearing the red and gold shield of the borough arms.

In the summer, cycling down Rainsford Lane, past Bruce's jam factory on the left side at Rainsford Road end and, a little further on, Mr Blyth's sweetshop, one reached Harry Medley's, a market gardener, which was later built over by cul-de-sac Norton Road. There, one could buy a fresh lettuce, or mustard and cress for tea.

At the bottom end, H J Taylor garaged his removal vans and nearby was a detached 'mystery' house, with tatty and dirty lace curtains, rumoured to be the home of a recluse. Until the early thirties, the River Can flowed across the Lane here, in a ford, with a narrow wooden footbridge. The name Rainsford Lane extended all the way up to Writtle Road, with just a half dozen houses at the top end. Halfway up, on the left, was Waterhouse Farm, hence the choice of name when the new road came into being, but even then, there was no way through for vehicles, only for pedestrians and cyclists. The passage of hundreds of cycles over the years had gouged a track - at times very muddy - between high clay banks and the Lane was just a stony track, on the edge of town. It was far from being a main artery to the centre, as now. Fields on either side were often flooded in winter time.

Returning to Rainsford Road, behind Webb's tailors and next to the long gardens of Critchett Terrace, was Mr Hora's garage. Right at the end of the terrace was little Mrs. Eve's tiny, unpretentious sweets and tobacco shop, with a low entrance to duck under and one step down. It was a favourite haunt of St Peter's choirboys, who spent their pocket money in there, before singing practice began.

Further on was St Peter's Infants' School and a petrol station was on the corner of Primrose Hill, just past Campen's builders yard. The tall petrol pumps, each with an illuminated globe at the top indicating the make, also had a little glass reservoir, which needed to be observed full of petrol before pumping began. A tiny propellor within the reservoir revolved as the petrol flowed, while an attendant wound a handle, pumping the liquid into the car, at the same time keeping an eye on the dial to ascertain how many gallons he had supplied.

On, on the corner of south Primrose Hill, the Misses Ireland kept a greengrocery for many years, having a display of vegetables on a forecourt and a short way along towards Roxwell Road, past private houses, there was a yard where Donald Denoon's displayed Ford tractors. An old, three storey warehouse, with an outside wooden staircase was next, where, in the empty top floor, St Peter's Players sometimes rehearsed. A confectioners, owned by a rather strait-laced lady, who kept a glass jar of violet cachous on the counter was below and a few yards further on were the private houses of dentist Mr Sellick and Doctor Harris. In Ardmore, a large house behind tall evergreen trees, with a double entrance drive, right next to Admirals Park, were Mr & Mrs Sidney C Taylor, sometime mayor and mayoress of the borough. He was a director of the *Essex Weekly News*. Between the end of the low front stone wall and park side entrance was the only red telephone box in the area. High wrought iron railings were in place along the whole front of the park and double gates were across the main entrance.

Across the other side of Rainsford Road lived Mr Escott, who had market stalls in Chelmsford and Braintree, while his wife sold goods at the back door. Sheds in the back garden stored toilet soap and powders, tinned foods, vinegar and sauces and in the house was an inviting selection of sweets for children who, like me, shopped there for their mothers on Saturday mornings. Their son, Ronald, eventually took over the market stall business.

Back towards the town was J C Pryke, one of three builders in this end of Rainsford Road (the others being G J Hawkes and Campens). Beside the Home School allotments and long stony drive up to the school were County Horticultural Gardens and their expert Head Gardener, Mr F W Shemming was in much demand for the interesting talks he gave on the subject to various societies. He also possessed a fine, rich baritone voice, which delighted audiences when he sang in concerts.

At the side of the Rose and Crown was a tiny cycle workshop, where bikes and punctures were repaired and solid rubber tyres fixed on children's fairy cycles, by very obliging George Page and his son. Mr Outten, who had a greengrocer's shop on the corner of School View Road, also sold vegetables from a cart, drawn by a ginger coloured horse, which we boys didn't much like, although he also sold delicious marshmallow cakes, which we cajoled our mothers into buying!

Brown's, a baker's, was on one corner of Maltese Road and on the other, in a charming thatched cottage, lived Ernest Rowland and his family, prior to their move to Great Baddow. Choirmaster Mr Peter Bush and his sister were residents of this quiet cul-de-sac, right next door to two of St Peter's choirmen, brothers Owen and Harold Parkins. The vicar of the parish lived in a large vicarage at the far end and St Cedd's private school occupied another spacious house.

Further along, on this side of Rainsford Road, was a parade of small shops, including, at various times, a hairdresser, confectioner, draper, fishmonger, men's outfitters, furniture store, laundry, cycle dealer, shoe repairer, herbalists, café and radio service, most of them changing hands and trading style over the years. A large advertising hoarding, behind a low fence and then Rainsford Methodist Church came between the shops and Cedar Avenue.

J Sainsbury's Chelmsford branch, 1931

BUSES, FROM STEAM TO M25

In the early 1900's, my father, Charles, who was an engineer, moved from Islington to Chelmsford with Thomas Clarkson, who owned a company making steam powered buses. They occupied premises in Moulsham, opposite St John's church, on the corner of Queen Street, the building later becoming Last's Garages. As well as working on construction of the chassis, Dad also drove them to the firm's London works, where they were equipped with bodywork and seating. The company adopted the name of The National Steam Car Company, one day to be renamed Eastern National.

The original high, brick omnibus station which was in due course built in Duke Street was mainly undercover and passengers queued in an orderly fashion until they spotted that their bus had turned into the back garage area, before swinging round to pull up beside them, when they clambered aboard. An inspector would be heard calling out, "Brownings Avenue", "Eves Corner", "Laindon" or some other destination, as a vehicle drove into view and people might occasionally have to run to where it stopped - not always in the anticipated spot. (Buses going as far as the corner of Chignal Road, off Roxwell Road, waited outside the station, on the road opposite the public toilets). When it was time to depart, a bus emerged directly into the roadway, between solid brick pillars that supported the roof - there were several exit points.

If a certain driver were seen to be in the bus, there would be a groan from the queue. "Oh no, it's Old Slowcoach!" He was a big man, with a large black moustache and drove rather slowly, so passengers knew it would take somewhat longer to get to their destination. He always wore a greatcoat buttoned up to the neck during cold weather and frequently had trouble getting the engine into gear - there would be many sarcastic, but good-humoured comments along the journey.

Early double deckers were all open topped, so when my brother and I boarded one of those to visit an uncle at Danbury, we always ducked our heads, gazing up at the scraped brickwork, as it drove under the low railway bridge! Two of those buses once took pupils from King's Road School on an outing to Maldon and near Danbury, my brother, who was sitting in front upstairs in the first vehicle had his school cap whipped off by a tree under which they were passing. But he didn't lose it - it dropped into the following bus!

All buses going through High Street first stopped in the roadway by the little island in the railway station forecourt, before turning right into Market Road, making another stop by Dr Alford's long garden wall and travelling round until emerging into Tindal Square, to the next stop in front of shops near the Shire Hall. Then off to a further halt at Springfield Road corner, in front of Macfisheries open fronted shop. If their route did not take them towards Springfield, next stop was at The Regent and either through narrow Moulsham Street or round into Baddow Road.

It seems incomprehensible that buses took that route, winding through Market Road, whereas when they returned, they drove directly up Duke Street, after stopping to pick up passengers waiting on the pavement in front of Judge Tindal (which was then in a more central position in the Square). The routes were later transposed to the more sensible direction, which did not involve outgoing buses having twice to cross the flow of traffic.

On the brickwork above the railway bridge was an advertising poster and the one that always seemed to be there was of a smiling, rosy cheeked man clad in blue and white pyjamas, with his arms and legs wrapped round a huge jar of Bovril, floating on a stormy sea, above the slogan, "Prevents that sinking feeling!" A permanent green and gold sign advertising L P Foreman & Son, timber merchants in Roxwell Road, later replaced it.

If passengers waited outside Wenley's for a bus emerging from Springfield Road and it went by full, some raced through the arcade, crossed the road and stood outside Dace's music shop to catch another one, perhaps from Baddow direction. This would have turned left at Baddow Road corner into Moulsham Street and right into The Friars, right again into London Road. Youngsters intending to travel to Broomfield or beyond might then alight at the Friends' Meeting House stop, run through the railway arch and jump on an Eastern National, or get on a Hicks bus, waiting by Donald Denoon's car showroom in Coval Lane. The fare as far as Patching Hall Lane was one (old) penny.

There was a conductor on every bus, to ring the bell, once for stop, twice for go (and occasionally three times, indicating 'full up'), pulling down on a cord suspended from the ceiling, which ran from the back into the driver's enclosed cabin. Conductors wore a leather money pouch that hung from a strap round the neck and carried different coloured tickets secured in a wooden holder by strong springs. Another essential piece of equipment carried was a machine to punch holes in tickets when they were issued, accompanied by a 'ting' from the punch. Children's conductor sets, complete with cap, badge, pouch and tickets in a holder, were very popular playthings on sale at toyshops.

In an improved system, brought out later on, conductors turned a handle on a machine that printed, then spewed out a strip of tickets. When a new roll of paper was needed, it was not uncommon to see a wasted strip blowing along the street, having been discarded by a conductor.

One notable Eastern National conductor kept passengers amused with a running commentary as the bus passed through town, announcing, for instance, the title of the film on at the Regent Theatre that day, along with precise information on exactly which stop had been reached. Such characters made the journey a happy one, imbuing passengers with a feeling of goodwill, if only for a while

Hick's dark blue double deckers, emblazoned with the company name in yellow came into town from Braintree, while Lodge's blue and cream coaches brought shoppers from High and Good Easter and the Roothings - the quaint name for the collection of nine villages named Roding. There were also Ashdown's brown painted buses, from Baddow.

Other coaches to take passengers to London had two departure points. Hillman's started off from the forecourt of the Rose and Crown, in Rainsford Road, while Primrose coaches, owned by local brothers named Rose and appropriately painted primrose yellow, picked up their passengers at the top of Market Road (Victoria Road South), again by Dr Alford's wall. Their main stopping place in London was at the Finsbury Park Astoria, in Seven Sisters Road, later named Rainbow Theatre.

Grey-Green coaches, covering a large part of the country, drove through Epping on the way from London and their customers might alight anywhere, from Roxwell to the centre of town. Empire coaches also came through, at one time, on their way from London to Norfolk.

Hillman's was owned by the proprietors of Maylands aerodrome at Harold Wood. This was a small airfield, now a golf course, and a group of us went there on an outing from King's Road School, in 1934, to see a flying display, including our first glimpse of parachutists. A special feature was the arrival from France, of Monsieur Dowg, in a tiny plane called the Flying Flea and it was a great thrill to secure his autograph after he landed. Sadly, a few years later, he was killed while flying the little aircraft.

Clarkson steam powered bus, 1907

AN OIL STOVE, DOCTORS AND A THIEF

The only heating in our Park Avenue house was from coal fires, in the living and 'front' rooms and, though very rarely, they might be lit in black wrought iron fireplaces in the two bedrooms. Wood needed chopping, coal had to be shovelled into a scuttle and ashes cleared daily. We had a piano in that seldom-used front room and when my brother had his weekly music lesson from Mrs Dawson, a black Valor oil heater would be lit in there during cold weather. Teacher Mrs Dawson had over a mile to walk back home, but never feared any danger on a dark winter's night.

The iron framed piano, which had come from my mother's old home, had a front panel, above the keyboard, decorated with a delicate gold filigree pattern and, on either side of the folding music stand was a brass candlestick, hinged so that it could be pushed back when not in use.

There were other traditional features in that room. Apart from several family photographs and 'Monarch of the Glen' type prints hanging on cords from the picture rail, an aspidistra in a jardinière stood on a circular table in the bay window. Leaning against one wall was a three-fold screen, its black fabric covering a wooden frame, with a gold embroidered Japanese pattern. Nearly six feet tall, it was intended for shielding occupants of the room from draughts.

Above the fireplace, both in here and the dining room, was a mirror surrounded by a wooden decorative framework, supporting shelves on which pairs of ornaments were displayed. The mirrors were both modernised in the mid-thirties. On the mantelpiece stood a green marble chiming clock, with an engraved brass plate denoting it was a wedding gift, on 6th June, 1908 to my father from colleagues at Clarkson's, the steam omnibus builders in Moulsham.

Another treasured item in there was an early nineteenth century musical box, which played six different tunes and was wound up by a lever at one end. It was fascinating to watch the drum revolve, while the hundred of needles on it 'plinged' against a musical comb, to produce different notes.

In the entrance hall was a wall-mounted hat rack, used by all the family, for everyone wore a hat, when going out. Even teenage boys sported a 'pork pie', which was a version of the trilby worn by older men and one has only to examine old photographs or newsreels of crowds at a football match, to verify that no head was uncovered, though the majority there wore flat caps. In church, every woman was required to have her head covered and most would never be seen in public without their favourite 'titfer'.

Beside the chimney in each of two bedrooms upstairs was a marble topped wash-stand, on which stood a toilet set of china basin, water jug and soap dish, all decorated in embossed pink rose pattern. They were ostensibly kept for use by visitors who stayed overnight, though probably remained because they were conventional bedroom ware and made the room look complete.

Because Monday was always washday, my mother produced a simple mid-day dinner using cold meat left over from the Sunday roast. We always had a sweet, often jam roly-poly, made with suet, or apple pie and custard. There's nothing like mother's puddings!

Breakfast was either Kellogg's or Force wheat flakes, though we sometimes had Post Toasties, a corn cereal originating, like Kellogg's, in America. Packets bore the signature of Mr C M Post, as did the oval shaped tins of my mother's bedtime drink, called 'Instant Postum'. This was somewhat similar to coffee, with small brown crystals to be dissolved in hot water. Another tasty breakfast cereal that became available was puffed rice, no longer seen in shops.

On packets of Quaker Oats, a warming porridge we ate in cold winter months, the Quaker trademark could be cut out and sent in the required numbers for free gifts - conjuring sets and 'disguise' outfits, including moustaches to be fixed on one's nose by a wire clip and ginger hair to make a beard.

Every summer, eggs were 'put down', an expression used to denote the method by which they were preserved for winter consumption. Mostly white, they were put into an enamel pail, covered in 'waterglass' and stored under a pantry shelf. This seems very strange now - and raises the question - did chickens not lay in winter?

On Wednesday afternoons, mother used to visit an old friend in Henry Road, off Rectory Lane, but if, for some reason she wasn't able to go, a card was posted, bearing a ha'penny stamp, before 9 am and it was delivered by second post at 11 am. There might even be a reply in the third post of the day, around five, delivered by a postman wearing a smart dark blue uniform with red piping and a hard hat, without a peak, similar to a navy fez. We had an early morning delivery every Christmas Day, too.

Postage increased in the early thirties to one penny for cards and three ha'pence for letters and stayed at those rates for some years. We very seldom received a telegram, but if one came, it was delivered by a boy wearing a navy uniform, similar to the postman, but with a little 'pillbox' cap.

Unlike today, the word 'sex' was never mentioned, even among my friends and there was never any instruction, either at home or school. When friend Bill Grew took his first job, on leaving school, at a hatchery, determining the sex of day-old chicks, that word was heard at home - and my mother sniffed disapprovingly. Similarly, another 'banned' word came into use with the arrival of a new popular song, which included the words, 'with her head tucked underneath her arm, she walked the Bloody Tower'. We thought we were being very saucy when we sang it, but the word had to be pronounced in a northern accent, as in 'goody'! George Bernard Shaw's play, *Pygmalion* caused a sensation, when Eliza Doolittle uttered that immortal line on stage – "Walk? Not bloody likely!" We very quickly picked up "O.K." from Hollywood films and integrated it into our language, as did countries worldwide, but at first the expression was frowned on by the older generation.

It was only on very rare occasions that the family was treated to a car ride in the country by visitors to our home and one of them had a car with a 'dicky', which my brother and I rode in. This was a compartment in the open, behind the passenger seats, a sort of boot, which opened up to reveal a couple of folding seats, facing forward. It was great fun, more especially in sunny weather.

In 1932, we were roller-skating in the road, prior to the arrival of our father for tea, when we heard the sound of an accident at the junction of Park Avenue with Rainsford Road. We sped down to have a look, only to see the unconscious figure of Dad lying with his head on the kerb, bleeding profusely from mouth, nose and ears. He had been knocked off his bicycle by a car and suffered a fractured skull. My worried mother, who had been cutting a loaf of bread for tea, went in an ambulance with him to Chelmsford & Essex Hospital in London Road, where he eventually fully recovered, thanks to the care and attention of doctors and nurses. When he was getting better and had been transferred from 'A' ward, the equivalent of today's Intensive Care, to recovery 'B' ward, he needed some means of entertainment. This was provided, in the shape of a large radiogram and records, loaned by a friend, which, of course, served to amuse other patients as well. There was no Hospital Radio at that time!

Nurses endured a much harsher routine then than exists today. Matron's rule was very strict and nurses on night duty had only two nights off each month. Charitable gifts of eggs (which were preserved in dustbins) and groceries were doled out to night staff in the hope that they would find time to cook them in between time spent attending to patients. Sometimes an egg and an orange each were deemed sufficient to sustain them through the night. They grumbled, of course, but were devoted to their hard but rewarding work.

A true story that never reached Matron's ears concerned a young probationer nurse in 1927 who was given an instruction that patient Mrs P should be given two drams of hydrochloric acid. She duly went to the urine test cupboard, where she knew the acid was kept and measured the required drop of liquid into a glass, handing it to Mrs P. A moment later, on going to the ice box (pre-fridge days) she found a bottle labelled, "diluted Hcl for Mrs P." The horrified nurse then broke a rule about not running in corridors, as she raced to the patient's bedside, to see her with glass in hand, about to sip the acid. Exclaiming "Don't drink that, I forgot to put any sugar in it," she grabbed the glass. "But I don't take sugar," was the reply. However by then, nurse had firmly moved it out of harm's way and later administered the correct dose. She endured several sleepless nights after that incident!

When the racecourse at Galleywood was still functioning, a State Registered Nurse from the hospital was selected to attend, to take care of any possible casualties among the jockeys or crowds. On almost the last occasion that races were held, the nurse's only patient, brought in to her tent by officials right at the end, after she had carefully packed away her sterilised instruments, was suffering from a nasty cut on his chin. He was reported to have been kicked by a bookie! The nurse soon sutured the wound and repacked her equipment, ready to be taken back to the hospital.

Our own family doctor was Dr C W Alford, who was an inveterate smoker, resulting in his grey moustache being heavily brown stained. He had a chauffeur to drive him on his rounds. For a small town, we were very well provided for by the medical profession, for other local GPs included Doctors Camps (who became Home Office Pathologist),

Beauchamp, Corner, Henry, Lister, Martin, Newton, Platts, Pirie, Pitts, Storrs, Whitley and Willcocks.

Adults did not speak openly about illnesses and neighbours might be heard whispering words like 'expecting' or 'consumption', but youngsters were not encouraged to ask questions, which added to the mystery. But there were some silly superstitions, such as, "If you touch the inside of eggshells, you'll get warts".

On looking out of a bedroom window one Sunday morning, we saw cups and saucers from the previous evening's supper on the ground outside. Dad had been painting and had left the window very slightly open and, after lifting that crockery off the draining board, a careful burglar had then climbed through, stealing my mother's handbag, purse and some fresh fruit from a bowl. When police arrived, led by the astute Detective 'Kruschen' Baker, he asked, "Have you looked down at the bottom of the garden?" Sure enough, there were mother's belongings, less her money, plus orange and banana peel and an apple core! The thief, well known to police had been busy elsewhere that night and was soon apprehended.

All street lamps were gas lit, with a mantle and pilot light. A clock regulated switching on time and a council employee would visit each lamppost, place his ladder against the cross bar at the top and climb up to wind the clock and reset the time, according to when darkness fell - they did not stay on all night. When they were changed from gas to electricity, they sometimes failed to light at the proper time - but we boys found that a hard kick did the trick! The new Mercury vapour lights, when installed on tall lamp standards on main roads, made everyone look green.

We did not go out to play on Sunday and after evening service at St Peter's Church in Primrose Hill, the family and a few friends would in summertime take a walk through sedate Tower Gardens, before returning home. When we played on other days, 'cowboys and Indians' was a favourite game - Westerns were popular at the cinema. Our 'weapons' were potato pistols, which had to be pressed into a potato to form a pellet, pea shooters (shriveled dried peas obtainable in packets from grocers had to be blown through a metal tube by a strong puff), or cap guns, which were favourite because of the noise they made and ones that took a roll of caps were best of all. We had balsa wood model aeroplane kits and, once assembled we had to wind long rubber bands attached to propellers, in order to fly them.

There were two occasional arrivals in the district which none of us boys desired. One was the dreaded 'fever ambulance', a wooden paneled vehicle in which unfortunate diphtheria or scarlet fever patients were taken off to the Isolation Hospital in Baddow Road. The other was 'Daddy' Everett, an elderly, severe looking gentleman, with white side-whiskers, who appeared to glare down at us from atop his high bicycle. We really had nothing to fear from him - he was the town's School Attendance Officer - but his very presence made us quake!

Every Christmas was spent with an aunt, uncle and two cousins, when we always played games, especially Dumb Crambo and charades, dressing up in clothes (especially furs) sought from adults' wardrobes. Traditionally, uncle rolled up his trouser legs, blackened his knees with burnt cork and wore a school cap in one scene! We really had to act each syllable and speak lines, made up as we went along, inviting the 'audience', at the end to guess the whole word.

One year we had a ship theme (SS *Wangul*) for the duration of the visit, everyone wearing a crêpe paper sailor hat bearing the name of his or her 'rank'. High spot was when 'King Neptune', decorated with seaweed (sent by a friend living at Walton-on-Naze) was hauled aboard, on the end of a rope, with a sack of presents.

We always had gazooters, later called gazoos, to play a tune on and tissue paper on a comb was a lot of fun for making a noise. Most boys owned a mouth-organ, which we learned to call harmonicas, when we heard Larry Adler playing one on the radio and we also had a jaw's harp, often mistakenly called Jews' harp, which only 'twanged' and were far from tuneful. Teenage parties included Sardines, Murder and pencil and paper games. There were always guessing games, too, where someone had first to go out of the room. That spirit of fun seems to have been lost today, parties consisting mostly of drinking and dancing.

The author in his apprenticeship

RAINSFORD END AND BRICKWORKS

On the left corner of Cedar Avenue, leading from Rainsford Road, used to be Sidney Caper's fruit shop, until Mrs Kingcome opened up there as a confectioner and on the right corner, Mrs Ling's Sunray Café was a handy venue for Grammar School boys needing a hot lunch. Some prominent local businessmen resided in this quiet thoroughfare, including the Spalding family, Arthur Andrews, undertaker and some time mayor, Stanley and Harold Hance (proprietors of Hasler & Hance), Gerald Chambers, playwright and accountant, Mrs Brittain Pash, Miss C M Alford (sister of the doctor), Alan Rippon (the newsagent), Cecil Hart FRCO, Cathedral organist, Grammar School master 'Pussy' Johnson and, later, John Sargeant, butcher.

Where the avenue joined Broomfield Road, on the left hand side was Fewells dairy, while on the right was up-market Pollard's Garages. Right next door, along towards Rainsford Road, was Dr Martin's surgery, beside dentist A C King; hairdressers, Pendrills ironmongers and other shops took us along to Hawkes Garage, owned by chubby Jack Hawkes, who carried out minor repairs, but mainly dispensed petrol to vehicles parked alongside the kerb. A long overhead pipe led from the pump, which was operated by working a handle back and forth. Matthews, a pork butcher adjoined Rainbow Wools, on the corner, though this had formerly been Newcombe's cycles. From there, back along Rainsford Road, Thompson's Ironmongers, who specialised in varieties of paint, occupied three adjoining shops, one of which had previously belonged to Major Jacobs OBE. While this white moustachioed gentleman drove a taxi, available for private hire, his wife looked after their shop, selling china, glass, toys and, in November, fireworks. There was once piano showrooms next, before high wooden gates across a short drive leading to Coval Works, where were F J French, builders. The house later became Strutt & Parker's office and had once been the residence of Judge Tindal. Ralph Rowe, butchers, was next to J E Britton, fishmongers, then, until he moved to Duke Street, watchmaker C J Gramlick adjoined John E Day, domestic ironmonger. Mr Day also drove a pale blue van, which toured the town and villages dispensing paraffin. A tap protruded from a tank at the rear of the vehicle, while various oil-stained measures balanced and rattled on a shelf below. His son, John took over the business in due course.

The County Hotel, including Freemasons' Hall was on the opposite side of the road, Prior's fish and chip shop being next door, then Frank Eaton's petrol station and Rippon's (later Morrison's) newsagent. Several wide steps led up to the ornate, grey frontage of the Pavilion Cinema, where audiences were accustomed to seeing the film breaking at least once during the programme, to the accompaniment of loud jeers!

On the corner of Coval Lane, Donald Denoon's large Ford car showroom often put on a free film show, consisting of cartoons, advertising and travel features. Coval Lane was then a cul-de-sac, flats standing across the bottom end, which was named Pryke's Drive. A short way down, on the left was Burgess Well Road, leading to Viaduct Road and a walk through, under railway arches, to the recreation ground. Not far from my home in Park Avenue, many happy hours were spent enjoying the delights of Admiral's Park, paddling in the shallow River Can and fishing for tiddlers and mudgudgeons, which were taken home in a jam-jar - and usually found to have died a couple of days later! My friends and I also encountered an occasional crayfish and we made small dams in the shallow water, using bricks that had fallen from an old bridge. It had no sides, but we often walked across it, to explore fields the other side.

A murky pond over there, surrounded by barbed wire and trees, was rumoured to have been caused by a bomb, dropped from a Zeppelin during the Great War and there were also some shallow trenches, in which we played. There was a proper bridge, with rails at each side, completing a walk to the park from the direction of Waterhouse Lane and finally, a narrow footbridge crossed the water at the far corner of the park.

There was just one isolated house, in the middle of those fields, inhabited by a family known to all we boys, named Porter, who on very rare occasions attended morning service at St Peter's Church. Mr Porter senior had rather a loud voice and when he joined in singing hymns, it was most noticeable he was not always in tune!

Most children would make for the six swings near the river - but Never on Sunday! It was park-keeper Mr Passfield's task, every Saturday evening, to remove the black, greasy hooks and place all the swings in his barrow, wheeling them away to be locked in a shed in Tower Gardens until Monday morning. A five person swing was chained and padlocked and games on the nearby cricket field were not permitted on Sunday, either.

After taking a walk along the river, away from the park, one reached a watermill, at the end of a muddy road, which was to be named Beach Drive. Beyond it were brick kilns and neatly stacked piles of red bricks – Beach's Brick Works, the Beach family living at the top of this road. All the earth round about was red coloured, including the roadway and further on was a narrow gauge railway, with tip-up trucks that brought the clay from deep pits, which was to be made into bricks. On Sundays, when workmen were not around, my brother and I sometimes played on this railway, pushing and riding on the trucks and little turntable, beside those dangerous pits. Our parents never knew!

Tower Gardens was where the Conduit came to rest, placed on a grassy mound, becoming a feature of the putting green, on which games could be played on payment to one of Mr Passfield's gardeners, of twopence, which covered the hire of a putter and golf ball and a scorecard. Tennis hard courts were another feature of these colourful, well kept gardens and a round wooden shelter, liberally decorated with graffiti, sported ample seating for courting couples - until they were asked to leave as darkness approached and gates were locked behind them.

NARKOVER AND STRAW HATS

"Are YOU an Old Narkovian?" Such a question might have been put to you in Chelmsford in the thirties and the answer from quite a few people would have been in the affirmative.

It was not a secret society, with special means of recognising other members, but a notorious 'school', which supported a charity, St. Peter's Kitchens, in Garrick Street, London. There, the money raised by Narkovians and 'school staff' provided down and outs with free meals, first aid, clothing and a ticket entitling them to a bed for the night.

So where was this unusual school, with its little grey book of strange rules, covering such subjects as fees, singing, temper, visiting days and washing dirty linen? I refer my readers to the pages of 'Beachcomber'.

Despite boasting a great many pupils and well-known Governors, such as Douglas Fairbanks Jnr., Jessie Matthews and the Marquis of Donegal, there were no school buildings and certainly no morning assembly. But becoming a pupil was easy, as many Chelmsfordians found when approached by one already enrolled - on payment of just one shilling.

Having joined, the next step was to get more pupils to join, you just had to persuade two friends to hand over one shilling each and you then became a 'nark'. Every time a certain number of pupils were enrolled, a higher rank was attained in the school. Three more and one became a 'fag', another five made you a Monitor and yet another five meant being promoted to Senior Pupil, by which time you had passed over a sum of sixteen shillings from new members. On attaining rank, you could put letters after your surname. For instance MNC signified 'Monitor, Narkover College'. All quite meaningless, but enough to raise curiosity and perhaps a new enrolment.

One could then climb in stages through Prefect, Junior Master, Senior Master and finally, having now cajoled a grand total of one hundred new members, one reached the status of Old Boy, receiving, as reward, a signed photograph and letter of congratulations from Ronald Frankau, Will Hay or Clive Brook - all stars of stage and screen.

College Rule No.12 specified, "Parties of senior boys visiting the village pub must be personally conducted by the Headmaster (Will Hay), for a small fee payable at the bar". Another rule affirmed that under no circumstances would any boy be allowed to take back to the school less than two bottles, except by special request of the Head!

Pupils could purchase a tie and blazer emblem, or even, for thirteen shillings, a large enamelled badge to mount on the car bumper and everyone was required to wear a smaller one in the lapel. All badges were in the shape of a shield, coloured red, white and blue, with gold lettering. Across the top appeared the words 'Up Narkover', while in the four quarters were a pickaxe, shovel, handcuffs and three broad arrows! Scrolled underneath appeared the rank of the wearer.

Copies of the college anthem, "Up the Old Narkovians", written by music masters the music hall artistes The Two Leslies - Sarony and Holmes, could be obtained from the school, price sixpence. Or for half-a-crown, you might have bought a record, entitled "Don't Do the Dirty on a Fellow Narkovian", by 'Morals Adviser' Ronald Frankau.

This was all happening long before the phrase 'card-board city' had been coined, when the homeless and hungry of London were being assisted by the generosity of Narkover members and a shilling (5p), was really worth having in your pocket.

It was a lot of fun for 'pupils', not only in Chelmsford, but also across the country, who joined the college and, it also was, hopefully, a source of comfort for some of London's less fortunates. Up Narkover!

There was another fad, which lasted for a year or so – 'collecting' straw hats. One actually just counted them, when being worn by men, which was quite common in summertime. Either boaters - flat hats with an all-round brim - or panamas, shaped like a trilby counted towards the total. Schoolgirls wearing boaters as part of their uniform, did <u>not</u> count and neither did hats on display in shop windows.

But there was a bit more to it than just counting. For some unfathomable reason, every time you saw one, you had to lightly lick the side of the right hand and thump it twice into the open palm of the left hand! It all sounds so ridiculous, but was very real in the pre-war thirties. Whoever thought that up?

People often seen in 1930s newspapers and cinema newsreels included aviation pioneers and personalities such as the Aga Khan, who was born in 1877 and was very loyal to Britain. Extremely wealthy and, like his grandson today, very involved in horse racing, he would be seen attired in morning dress and top hat, often leading in his winning horse. Other pictures annually showed him being weighed in gold, which we were told would then distributed to poor Ismaili Mohammedans. As he was quite a big man, there must have been a lot of gold.

When aviation pioneers flew, especially the ladies, their exploits were closely followed on maps in the newspapers. In 1934, Jean Batten flew solo from Australia to England and back again. Four years earlier, twenty-two year old Amy Johnson had flown her little Gipsy Moth bi-plane from London to Australia and had been awarded the CBE by George V. An American, Amelia Earhart, was the first female to fly alone across the Atlantic, but later disappeared over the Pacific. Amy, the country's favourite airwoman, married Jim Mollison, another famous flyer she had met in Australia, and they later flew together across the Atlantic, earning a 'ticker-tape' welcome in New York.

Memories of more disturbing news remain. A man named Bruno Hauptmann, whose trial and eventual execution occupied the front pages for some while, kidnapped American Colonel Lindbergh's son. The colonel was another pioneer flyer, who had flown the Atlantic solo in 1927.

George V died in 1936 and the news came over the wireless at 7.30 am. We had become so used to having bearded King George and Queen Mary, with her rather haughty look and always wearing a peculiar hat, called a toque. They had been on the throne since 1910 and only the year before his death we had celebrated the Silver Jubilee, children receiving a 'silver' medal; on the reverse side of which were the words, "Borough of Chelmsford, Sidney C Taylor Mayor". We had also enjoyed a day off school.

There was then much respect for the monarchy, who remained remote and not expected to mix with commoners. The Queen named a new liner after herself, which had been known simply as number 534. It had remained on the stocks of a Clyde shipyard for a long time, while disputes and strikes prevented its completion. After its launch, cardboard kits were on sale, enabling children to construct 2 foot long colourful models of the liner.

"Teddy", the new king, who succeeded his father, was very popular and the scandal over his affair with Mrs. Simpson did not receive the amount of press publicity it would have today. Many people were sad when he abdicated, but we were soon enjoying the festivities of the coronation of his brother, George VI.

CHRISTY'S TO ST PETER'S

At one end of King's Road, immediately before it joined Broomfield Road, was an entrance to Christy & Norris's Ironfoundry, where items such as cast iron manhole covers - often to be seen in Borough roadways - were produced. Christy Brothers was next door, fronting the main road. They were electrical and radio engineers and their special feature was an excellent wireless relay system. Wires conducted around the nearby Boarded Barns Estate and other parts of the locality led into houses, where it was necessary to have only a simple loudspeaker and switch, to be able to tune into the two BBC radio stations then available. An inexpensive rental paid for the service.

The other end of King's Road terminated at an uncultivated field, just past a turning named after Mr Leonard Fell Christy, mayor from 1930 to 1932 - Christy Avenue, leading to The Green. This field, beside some allotments, was a real child's haven in the summer, when the grass had been cut. My playmates and I would heap up the sweet-smelling hay to make dens, pretend castles or trenches and spend hours happily playing there, or in our caves in the hedgerow at the side. It has all been built over since then, by an extension to King's Road.

Leading from this field was a narrow, uneven pathway known as The Squeezer, bordered by the high fence of Hoffmann's sports field one side and trees and a ditch on the other, behind gardens of Tower Avenue. It wound its way down to where Rainsford Road and Roxwell Road met, just opposite the big, red brick water tower, next to where Mr Passfield, the park-keeper and his family lived. They, like others living nearby, must have been so accustomed to the incessant 'chunt-chunt' of the huge pump, that they hardly heard it. At one side of the tower was Tower Gardens, on the other part of Admiral's Park was fenced off in the thirties to create a fine cricket field, complete with pavilion. Mr Passfield and his staff looked after them all.

One of my friends, like me, was a choirboy at St Peter's Church, Primrose Hill, where we attended practices three evenings every week. It is not uncommon for older choirboys to bully newcomers - and St Peter's was no exception, so it was a relief to become a senior boy! But my three years there, from the age of nine, were quite enjoyable. As every choirboy knows, he not only sings hymns, psalms, anthems and carols, but also becomes immersed in church ceremonials. Many boys at St Peter's, when their voices broke, became 'servers', carrying out altar rituals at services and as it was 'high church', incense was often in use. Singing at weddings was financially rewarding (just one shilling), although helping the vicar at christenings, by setting up chairs for godparents, fetching the water and uncovering the font, was not!

Occasionally visiting country churches, such as Willingale, in the summer, when choir and congregation travelled in special buses, to join in with the host church at evensong was a welcome diversion. Most memorable of these outings was to Margaretting, where we all had to walk across the main railway line, to reach the church. There were also the annual Festivals of Nine Lessons and Carols and 'The Passion According to St Matthew' which we sang at Easter. On very rare occasions, the congregation would be given a singing lesson, with great good humour, by the choirmaster, learning when to stand up and join in - an attribute often lacking in many churches. When he left the organ to conduct the choir, we sang unaccompanied.

Mr William Peter Bush ARCO, who was the highly respected choirmaster and organist, handed out my much appreciated choirboy pay, which advanced from one and sixpence to six shillings per quarter, personally. Mr Bush, who was familiarly known by either of his Christian names, began at the church in 1900, celebrated his fifty years with a great gathering of past choir members, church wardens and clergy at a special service in 1950 and again, for his Diamond anniversary, ten years later - a record of sixty years. He died in 1966.

He had conducted other choirs in the town and owned James Dace & Son, in London Road, once the only music shop around. He knew just about everything there was to know about music - and gave me a book of 'country boy' monologues, which he suggested I should perform at concerts.

Each year a Nativity Play was presented, when St Peter's was converted into a theatre, a stage being constructed at the west end, complete with full lighting and curtains - every Players' production was treated professionally. On one occasion, the vicar's wife, Mrs. Morgan had written the play, entitled *St Nicholas Shows the Way* and before each such event, the cast of shepherds, kings and sometimes angels or Roman soldiers would be required to attend at the Vicarage for a costume fitting. Nothing about the production was ever second rate - no tea cloths would be used as shepherds' headdresses!

There was an annual treat, for the combined choirs of both parish churches, to Clacton, when we had the day to enjoy the pier amusements, especially the glass maze, slot machines with working models and Steel Stella, a small blue and silver roller coaster. Then we all met at a café for tea, before returning to Chelmsford by coach. Sunday School treats, to Clacton or Walton-on-Naze, were also regular events, though it was not unknown for children to choose which church to attend - a C of E or other denomination - according to the reputation of its yearly outing!

At St Peter's, choirboys wore black cassock, white surplice and stiff collar with a black bow and in 1935 ladies, dressed all in blue, were a welcome addition to sing beside the choirmen. Two of them, Phyllis Cass and Joan Mason, were daughters of shopkeepers in the town.

The outside of St Peter's church was clad in cream painted corrugated iron, with a red roof, but inside, one would never have guessed that it was not more substantial, heavy wooden beams supporting the roof and wood panelling lining the walls. A single bell, housed on the rooftop, was far from tuneful when tolled to call people to worship, or when rung during Holy Communion services, at the same time as a gong was struck beside the altar, while bread and wine were being consecrated. In the twenties and early thirties, the slight frame of Charlie Bearman would be seen entering the green door of the organ chamber before a service, to prepare to pump air into large bellows, which provided wind for the organ - not an easy task. An electric pump one day supplanted him and the organ itself was modernised, with additional pipes and an elaborate keyboard.

The church and small St. Peter's Infants School (also used as junior Sunday School) beside it, were demolished some years ago, to make way for an office block, but a new Church of the Ascension was first built in Maltese Road, almost opposite the Vicarage.

The sister church of the parish, All Saints, on Boarded Barns Estate, was not consecrated and the chancel and altar were frequently screened by heavy blue curtains, so as to turn the body of the building, which included a kitchen, into a hall, where concerts, scouting activities, weekly Women's Guild and Mothers' Union meetings and other social events were held.

The Rev Ashley Turner, a dearly loved vicar of the parish for several years, once said to me, "Every white person should have to marry a black one, then there would be less strife in the world." That same statement was made in a religious progamme on TV in 2000 - over sixty years later!

St Peter's Church

HOFFMANN'S, WIRELESS AND CINEMAS

When what we then called the fire hooter sounded, it could be heard all over Chelmsford and men would immediately be seen running or cycling madly to the fire station in Market Road, to take up their duties. But that was not the only siren sounded in the town, as Hoffmann's, Crompton's and Marconi's, too, had their daily hooters, both at clocking-on and leaving off times.

At mid-day and 5.15 pm, New Street came alive, as hundreds of cyclists rode over the cobbles and crossed the sunken railway lines leading from the goods yard behind houses in Victoria Road directly into Marconi works. Through the narrow railway arch, or up Rectory Lane, furiously pedalled the men and women, speeding home for a hastily eaten 'dinner', or at the end of the working day, for their tea.

Many buses had also lined up, in Rectory Lane and New Street, to take workers to destinations near their homes. My father, who by the mid-thirties was a Departmental Manager, preferred to come home for his midday meal, so he regularly boarded one of the buses. But, as we were almost at the end of the journey, he had just half an hour to eat, before standing outside the house, with others living nearby, ready to board the bus taking them back to work. The system worked very well for many years

Like his father - and other family members - Dad had eventually gone to work at Hoffmann's, after leaving Clarkson's steam bus company and he joined the cricket team. When they played away, families were encouraged to go along to support them and a photograph was taken of everyone sitting in an open top charabanc, outside the Shire Hall, before moving off to watch the match. Other works outings were organised, including a visit to Croydon, London's only airport at the time, where we were allowed close inspection of *Scylla*, then the largest airliner in operation. It was a twin-engined biplane, made by Short's, very small compared to today's monsters of the skies.

Some Hoffmann factory workers could be recognised by the greasy smell that clung to their clothing and it was detectable even in the roads round the factory. It was not exactly objectionable, just a fact of life that we accepted. As in nearly every workplace, there were some well known characters at Hoffmann's, among them Sister Aitken, a martinet who ruled the factory First Aid section with a rod of iron. She would stand no nonsense or feeble excuses from the men who went to her with cuts and bruises - and dressings that needed changing were ripped off without hesitation. Always wearing a blue headdress, like a hospital matron, she smelled strongly of iodine! Her surgery was just inside the Rectory Lane archway, beneath a prominent clock.

Beside their factory, Hoffmann's built a well-appointed recreation centre, including a concert hall and billiard rooms and the great snooker ace, Joe Davis was once invited to play there. Sir Malcolm Campbell, who had broken the land speed record, driving his 'Bluebird' at more than 300 mph (and also broke records in his speedboat) was another invited guest, who enthralled audiences, talking about his experiences.

In 1921, the Duke of York, later King George VI, decided to bring together two hundred boys from public schools and a similar number from industry, at an annual camp at Southwold, Suffolk. They had to be about eighteen years old and be selected by their college or employer and in 1938 two Hoffmann apprentices were chosen to attend. They enjoyed a whole week of fun, including singsongs, notably 'Underneath the Spreading Chestnut Tree' in which the King participated, with suitable arm actions, plus plenty of sporting activities, films and amateur concerts

At a concert presented by some very talented Hoffmann employees in their large hall, celebrated singer Monte Rey was guest artist, performing his hit song, 'Donkey Serenade'. Aged ten, I was very thrilled when he autographed my programme. Employee Charlie Wood, appearing in the same show, had very cleverly constructed a xylophone, made entirely of Hoffmann ball bearing steel races, expertly tuned, on which he played Offenbach's 'Tales of Hoffmann', to enthusiastic applause.

Despite his Latin sounding stage name and choice of songs, Monte Rey was actually a Scotsman. He moved to Galleywood with his lovely wife, Maisie, where they had a smallholding, on which they kept chickens. Later in life he joined Chelmsford Spiritualist Society, where he insisted on being addressed by his real surname - Fyffe. He ended his days as guest of a Laird in a Scottish castle.

A representative of Hoffmann's who visited New York, brought back for my father a souvenir of the then tallest building in the world, the Empire State, which had been opened in 1931 - the very same building we had been thrilled to see King Kong 'climbing' at the cinema. An American propelling pencil, with four retractable colours, was given to me.

In a large house in Beehive Lane lived E K Cole, who set up a factory in Southend, manufacturing wireless sets under the trade name of EKCO. His home was fitted with a radio in every room and it eventually became a social centre for Marconi workers.

In those happy, pre-TV days, families gathered round the wireless in the evenings. Our set had two black Bakelite dials, one for volume control, and the other to select a station – 'wavelengths' was something we knew nothing about. These were positioned on the front of a homemade cabinet, containing glass valves and a lot of wires. On top stood a horn-shaped speaker and in a cupboard below were two batteries, a 'dry' one, about 10" x 6" and a 6-volt 'accumulator', which regularly had to be taken to a shop for recharging. In the back garden was a 16 foot pole, from the top of which a cable led to the house, down to an aperture in the dining room window frame, round a picture rail and finally to the wireless set. This was the most essential aerial, without which there would not have been reception.

Wireless sets on sale in shops were available at widely different prices, varying from a Benbow Junior crystal set for two guineas to an Efecsaphone Wireless Receiving Set at over £100 - an extremely expensive figure in 1925. It had 5 valves and incorporated an aerial to 'enable reception for up to 5 miles from a broadcasting station', although terminals were provided to connect to an outside aerial for a wider choice, 'including Continental' and for headphones. The set was an impressive piece of furniture, made in Jacobean oak and below the loudspeaker was a cupboard, fashioned to appear as four drawers, to accommodate a six-volt accumulator, 100-volt high tension battery, a 15-volt grid battery and headphones. An outside aerial was included in the price.

We mainly listened to the two BBC stations then available, but when we had a more modern set, an Ultra, with push buttons, my brother often tuned into Radio Luxembourg, a station sponsored by advertisers. 'DDD Prescription' was one of the frequently publicised products, as were Carters Little Liver Pills. A jingle that became very familiar was "We are the Ovaltiney's". Pop music had not then arrived and we enjoyed jazz, hill-billies and songs like Little Man, you've had a Busy Day and Umbrella Man, by Flanagan & Allen. Ukulele-playing George Formby, singing Chinese Laundry Blues and Leaning on a Lamppost, was a popular performer. The Mills Brothers, an American group singing in harmony, were also favourites.

On Saturday evenings, the BBC broadcast a programme that began with the words, "Stop! Once again we halt the roar of London traffic, to meet some of the interesting people who are IN TOWN TONIGHT." This was followed by Saturday Night Music Hall, with stars such as Elsie & Doris Waters, Scotsmen Harry Lauder and Will Fyffe, 'Headmaster' Will Hay, Mabel Constandurous ('Ma Buggins') and comedian Nosmo King, who took his stage name from a sign in a railway carriage (No Smoking). Gracie Fields and the Western Brothers were never to be missed, nor was Monte Rey!

Every weekday around five o'clock, Jack Payne and his band played the music of the time, but then Henry Hall's orchestra took over the programme slot. This was our high spot of the day, until father came home from work and we had to switch off. Our choice of music was not to his liking!

Canadian Carroll Levis and his Discoveries was another well-liked programme, when newfound talented singers and musicians were given the opportunity to perform on air, many years before Hughie Green's televised Opportunity Knocks. But few people knew that there was a Nurse Levis at Chelmsford Hospital, who was actually a cousin of Carroll's.

Broadcasting had begun at Marconi's and their two 450 ft radio masts dominated the local skyline for years. When we saw them - and a smaller one in Hall Street - being taken down, section by section, by some intrepid steeplejacks, we felt that a little bit of history was disappearing, too. They had become so familiar; we just could not believe they were no longer necessary.

There were formerly five town cinemas, but the Empire in Springfield Road was closed down and demolished. The Select was commonly known as the Fleapit and the Pavilion was a simple, rectangular building, without a balcony, but with an impressive frontage. The Ritz, built on land between Baddow Road and the River Can was not able to have an electric Wurlitzer organ rising majestically from below the stage, because, so we were told, damp from the riverside would have affected it. However, before the programme commenced, we were treated to a dazzling display of coloured lights, reflected on ruched curtains that filled the proscenium arch, dimming and changing in an exciting sequence that was new to the town.

The cinema was later renamed the Odeon and dances were held in its ballroom, adjoining the restaurant. Before the arrival of the Ritz, a circus and a fair came to town every year and set up in King's Head Meadow. Carnival fireworks took place there, too, until the venue was moved to the Rec. The famous Bertram Mills Circus, which performed annually at Olympia, in London, was an attraction that sometimes came to thrill us.

The Regent had been a music hall and retained many of the old trappings, such as a box each side of the proscenium and gilt decorative plasterwork throughout. As mentioned elsewhere, Chelmsford Amateur Operatic and Dramatic Society put on annual musical productions there until 1939, having performed, in their early days, at the old Empire. A prominent warning notice one day made an appearance on each side of the screen, 'SILENCE – TALKIES' and a sign in the foyer announced 'SOUND BY WESTERN ELECTRIC'.

There were just two film classifications, A for Adults only and U, which meant Universal - all ages. Cinemas were not open on Sundays, but on Saturday mornings, programmes of films suitable for children were shown, entrance sixpence. *Tarzan*, with Johnny Weismuller, who appeared in 1935, had every boy trying to imitate his warning call to wild animals. Other favourites were Harold Lloyd, Charlie Chaplin, Laurel & Hardy or Tom Mix in a 'cowboy' film. The supposed exploits of these and other film stars were chronicled every week in *Film Fun*, a children's periodical. A story about the Great War, *All Quiet on the Western Front* is remembered for the exciting dogfights between British and German bi-planes we saw on screen. We little knew that we would one day witness the real thing, taking place almost over Chelmsford.

There was no such thing as continuous performances, so we queued at a cinema for the start of a programme and were marshalled in by a uniformed commissionaire, then shown to our seats by an usherette. There was a regular order to what we expected to see. After some advertising, a B film and a cartoon - Felix the cat was succeeded by Mickey Mouse and Donald Duck - came Pathé Pictorial, or Movietone News and then a trailer for the next week's film, commonly called the 'coming shortly's'. Finally, we watched the 'big' picture. If any of the minor items were missing, we felt cheated and would warn our friends about it, but we certainly enthused to find the film we had gone to see was a 'talkie'!

People often seen in newsreels included author and playwright George Bernard Shaw, pictured at his home in Ayot St Lawrence, though sometimes this eccentric Irish literary gentleman, with a white goatee beard and 'plus fours' tucked into his long woollen socks was made fun of in newspapers and newsreels. Sporting heroes were worshipped by many, especially people like cricketers Jack Hobbs and Don Bradman, whom every schoolboy wielding a bat on the lawn or in front of a lamppost imagined himself to be. Boxer Tommy Farr was another sportsman whose career was keenly followed, as was the American Heavyweight champion, Joe Louis.

Nowadays, we are accustomed to hearing of multiple births, but in the thirties, the arrival of quads at the sleepy village of St Neots, by the A1 in Huntingdonshire, was startling news and we followed the children's progress for years. But there was a sad occasion, one Sunday morning in 1930. My parents had often told the story of a German Zeppelin they had seen come down in flames near Billericay, in 1916, during the Great War and showed us the souvenir pieces of fabric and metal from it they had recovered. So the adventures of two British airships, R100 and R101, were very real to us. But the latter, the largest airship in the world, crashed in France, with the loss of all on board. So ended British dreams of this type of transport becoming popular.

BADDOW ROAD TO THE FRIARS

The entrance to Loveday's jewellers (later owned by Bickell's) on the corner of Baddow Road was in Moulsham Street and on the wall above the first floor windows was a large, black-faced clock, with gold figures and hands, the time on it being visible from the Stone Bridge. Right next door was Chelmsford Star Co-op men's and boy's outfitters. Privately owned outfitters, including S & S Sams, which sold Army surplus gear, Hancock's and Jolley's and Mrs Fincham's wool shop were in this section, as were Barker's bakery, De'ath furnishers and the Nag's Head pub. Builders W H Fincham were also based here at one time.

Harold Catling, who formerly dealt in carpets, was at number eleven, before he opened the very popular Sunbeam Café, by Wood Street roundabout, now Miami Grill. On one corner of Mildmay Road was Charles Boreham's cycle shop and on the other, a tyre dealer, Godfrey's. Several private houses along the road were interspersed with businesses, including Lee's laundry, a shoe repairer and Bullock's coal office. There was also a Congregational Church and Mr T E Howes hairdressers. Tommy Howes took office as mayor and later was chairman of the Carnival Association for some years.

Lynmouth Avenue did not exist before 1931, but placed among several private houses along this part of Baddow Road, which had no numbers, only names, and Elnaugh's electrical engineers was well established. A J Abraham's nursery was demolished to make way for Kenning's Motors, next to Goldlay House, the pillared residence of Ernest Copland Gray Esq. a local JP. His house was to become the business premises of T Betts and Co, who for well over sixty years provided yeast, cake decorations, fruit and other commodities to bakers throughout Essex, delivered by their fleet of brown vans.

Goldlay Avenue is another 'new' road, although J Gard timber merchants existed before 1930. But the Army & Navy public house was formerly located further along, towards Baddow, before being built next to Gard's, on the corner of Van Dieman's Road - part of what used to be known as the Arterial Road, or Chelmsford's by-pass. It was opened by Prince George, a son of George V, who named the section from there to Widford, Princes Road. He was later made Duke of Kent and was married to the favourite Royal of that time, elegant Princess Marina.

Across the road, returning towards town was Marriage's Mill and some cottages, long before John Sadd's showroom appeared. Simmons' (printers), Trigg & Moore, builders and one or two small businesses completed this area of Baddow Road, prior to the arrival of the Ritz cinema.

Moulsham Street, proceeding from Loveday's corner shop, hardly changed over the years, with a branch of W & O Budd bakers, Osborne's tobacconist and Ryder's toyshop being prominent. The latter could truly be termed a family business, as, apart from Mr & Mrs George Ryder, both of their sons, Doug and Reg and daughter Joan joined the firm on leaving school. The Windmill Inn adjoined Ralph Catt's grocery Store, Fulcher's florists and another branch of Bellamy's chemists. Mr T H Grew operated the town's only pawnbroker, opposite The Friars.

Eileen Holberton, who ran a ladies' hairdressers here, was a former Chelmsford Carnival Queen and Frank Poney, baker and pastry cook, opened a branch, which used to be Nickelsons. The Salvation Army Citadel, on the corner of Hall Street, came alive with navy blue uniformed, happy worshippers every Sunday and their tuneful brass band was always a joy to hear, often playing for their service in Tindal Square and touring the town just before Christmas to entertain with carols. Further along, a branch of Cramphorn's managed by Mr Double, offering food and bedding for household pets, plants and breakfast cereals, was on the corner of Orchard Street.

So many old businesses along here no longer exist. There once were a horse slaughterer, a boot maker, a branch of Luckin Smith's grocery and a lodging house for down and outs, where a man died when it caught fire. There were ugly rumours and accusations over that incident. Miss Mullucks kept a confectioners, Mr Fairbrass a fruiterers and there was a similar shop, kept by Walter Fincham, only a few doors away. The Misses Smee sold ladies' hats and Joe Willingham made ropes. H & T C Godfrey's tents were always in demand at open-air public events and their factory was between Grove Road and Hamlet Road, their principal shops being in Duke Street and Tindal Square.

St. John's School, beside St John's Church were, appropriately, almost on the corner of St John's Road, where, in the first house, lived Geoff Waring, who became editor of the *Essex Weekly News* and, next door, Miss Edith Stock ran a small private school at her home.

Further along upper Moulsham, near the junction with New London Road, several large houses on both sides of the road, with names, but no numbers, were the residences of some prominent citizens. Oaklands Park, complete with tennis courts, also housed the Borough Museum, which I visited a number of times over the years and always found most uninspiring, with the same old dreary exhibits, but it has now been made more inviting.

Returning towards the town centre, on the opposite side, were several terraced almshouse cottages, on a level raised several feet higher than the roadway, necessitating a correspondingly higher pavement and guard rail. On the corner of Queen Street was Lasts garage, mentioned in another chapter, adjoining Grovic sack depôt, which was converted, in the mid thirties, to T Wall & Son's local ice cream depôt.

After Anchor Street, two pubs, not far apart, were the Anchor and Star & Garter, surrounded by shops which changed hands several times – Thursby's furniture became Matthews pork butcher, Hawkes Bros sweetshop was taken over by Mr Tye, Harold Frear took Burn's hardware store, George Orrin's shoe repairers became R E French and Mrs. Coombs fishmongers was formerly Brown's.

Ernie Evans' printing shop was also where one could register with National Deposit Friendly Society. Before starting a first job, after leaving school, we needed to get a card, from an office such as this, on which an employment stamp was fixed each week by the employer, who paid part of the value, the employee paying the rest. There were sufficient spaces on the card for one year's use, when another one would be issued. On leaving a job, the card and any subsequent ones filled with stamps, would be returned to the person leaving, ready to be handed over to a new employer. This is how the - now hardly used - saying originated, should his boss sack a person, "I've got my cards."

Along this stretch of road, two shops stand out; Priors, double fronted, was noted for excellent fish and chips and Gibson's was a large furniture showroom, owner Mr G H Gibson's elder son, Donald one day becoming a very active town councillor. Denny the draper occupied two adjoining premises, on the corner of New Writtle Street. Moore's furniture, a small amusement arcade, Green's butchers, Bata shoes and a host of other assorted businesses brought one to the corner of Friars Place, commonly known simply as 'The Friars'.

In the twenties, a tailor's stood on that corner, then next door in Friars Place came Miss Dowsett's baby wear, Orrin's shoe repairs, a cycle dealer and Frank Tunbridge's Friars Temperance Hotel. Towards London Road were some private houses and Regent Garage; right opposite were more houses, Friars Council School and, on the corner with Moulsham Street, was Warwick Preston, Surgical Appliance maker.

In the short distance in Moulsham Street between The Friars and Bonds furnishing showroom were Friary Fruit and Veg., Royce ladies' hairdressers, Joseph Mason's second bookshop (the other being in Duke Street), managed by his daughter, Joan, a branch of Hugh Wright's and three more little shops.

So many of these old buildings, just like those in Tindal Street, were swept away in the cause of progress and modernisation. Even memories of them will soon disappear, too.

EMPIRE THEATRE TO LONDON ROAD

Along Springfield Road, close to its junction with High Street and next to Fifty Shilling Tailors was the most notable china shop in town, Collins, where a wide range of full sets of dinner and tea services and glassware were on offer. Mr Jack Collins himself was always on hand to offer advice. A few doors further along was the Labour Exchange, next to the site of the demolished Empire Theatre, which had stood beside the river in Springfield Road for many years, first as a theatre, before changing to films. It was rumoured that rats ran across patrons' feet while they were watching a programme! This was where Brown & Sons timber merchant's showroom was built. They had taken over a similar company, Wray & Fuller, some years previously.

A short distance further on, The Two Brewers public house was another of the old pubs around town, in several of which, games such as dominoes, shove-ha'penny and darts were provided for customers to enjoy. Sewell & King's garage and car showroom was on the corner of Navigation Road, next to County Laundry and W & O Budd's bakery. Behind Navigation Road was an unloading dock for Brown's timber yard, at Springfield Basin. Horse-drawn barges, having negotiated several locks on the Chelmer and Blackwater Canal could there be seen bringing coal for the Gasworks and Norwegian timber for Brown's, which had all been unloaded from ships which arrived at Heybridge Basin.

Opposite Victoria Road and on the corner of cul-de-sac Weight Road, the imposing Three Cups public house, with its prominent three large brass cups displayed high up on the sign, dominated this part of town. Between the pub and Johnson's grocery, on the corner of Trinity Road, were a barber, shoe repairer and Waskett's fish shop. On taking the steep rise into Trinity Road, immediately past Holy Trinity Church, on the left side, was Trinity Road School, where boys were separate from girls. But teachers were not kept apart, for Headmistress Miss Brown married the Headmaster, Mr Hutchinson.

Deputy headmistress, Miss Jeffkins, formed a group of handbell ringers, who were sufficiently competent to be invited to entertain audiences outside school and were particularly appreciated by clubs for blind people. Other teachers included Miss Selby, who taught gymnastics, the Misses Brittain, Mance, Reading and Mundy. Mr Maguire, school dentist, was often on duty here, in a well-equipped surgery, to attend to children needing treatment from the borough's Council schools. He also had a practice in town.

The church and its large graveyard were bordered on one side by the prison wall of Chelmsford Gaol. A 1930's vicar, the Rev Hopkirk, was such a remarkable preacher that congregations at his services not only occupied every seat, but also stood in the aisles to listen to his sermons. How many other parsons could attract such a following?

Springfield Park Road, part of a new estate of identical, grey pebble dashed houses built in the thirties and often referred to as 'The Allied', after the name of the builder, was an extension of Trinity Road. Between it and Sandford Road was wasteland, used as a playground by local children, but in 1932, a group of prisoners, supervised by warders began building a high wall around the area and it became part of the prison. One or two estate tenants secreted an occasional cigarette for the prisoners!

In Springfield Road, way past the Chelmsford Gaol and Sandford Road, some large houses were the homes of several prominent citizens, including Hugh Wright MBE, the Bellamys, Bolingbrokes, Ridleys and F Luckin Smith. On the opposite side, the Rt. Rev H A Wilson, Lord Bishop of Chelmsford, lived at Bishopscourt, on the corner of Stumps Lane, his house not visible from the road, being screened by high trees and evergreens. On more than one occasion, garden parties held here were entertained by Miss Doris Rodd's Dancing School, the young ladies dancing on a lawn.

Returning towards town, the Co-op had a grocery shop on the corner of Arbour Lane, next to Miss M E Ratcliff's private prep. school and several other businesses existed along this side, in between private houses. These included two butchers, Hugh Wright and Copsey, Luckin Smith grocery, Ward's newsagent and Essex Arms public house. Cramphorn's had a branch on the corner of Victoria Road, while on the opposite corner, Essex Rivers office was established in the mid-thirties.

There were further small shops interspersed with houses along this side, for instance, a branch of Budds bakers and a Ralph Catt, grocers. Much respected Doctors R W Willcocks and R E Pitts lived and practiced a few houses apart, not far from Rosebery Temperance Hotel. Businesses in Rosebery yard on several occasions changed hands - at times there was a scale maker, battery manufacturer, wholesale fruiterer, blacksmith and Carter Paterson, national carriers, whose green lorries were a familiar sight around town.

Towards Springfield Road corner was a Hawkes Bros. sweetshop, Broom Collier, draper and a small gents' hairdressers, which had no electricity, therefore the barber could not employ powered clippers, but instead could be seen using lighted tapers to singe his customers' hair. Close by was Gray & Sons brewery and finally, the Black Boy public house.

Turning right past the white Conduit and travelling up High Street brought us, on the left side, to London Road and to some more important shops just around the corner. On the left was an entrance door to F Luckin Smith grocery and, when Wenley's frontage was redeveloped it included other businesses, such as Edna Duffield's high-class florists, J Cowan Gowns and a men's outfitters.

Passing over the River Can on this side, via the green Iron Bridge, brought us to London Road Congregational Church and a number of private houses, including that of Dr Slaughter, an unfortunate name for a surgeon! After Friars Place was J B Slythe, monumental mason, whose display of white crosses and headstones visible from the hospital opposite was not readily appreciated by ill patients! Alongside Windley Bros. engineering works and Youngs coachbuilders was an entrance to the roller skating rink. Finally, Eastern Autos car showroom took us to the corner of New Writtle Street.

On the same side, several private houses, four road junctions, Harry Pigg's Red Lion, St Margaret's private school and Lucking Undertakers (with a Nonconformist cemetery at the side) led to The White House, which was the last in New London Road. Opposite was the Rising Sun, always a bus stop for Eastern National.

Travelling down that side, one came to Fanum House, local office for the Automobile Association on the corner of Writtle Road. Further on lived Fred Spalding, just before St

Phillip's Priory, which was a Convent High School for girls and Kindergarten for little boys. John Ockleford Thompson's house and St Anne's Preparatory School were also along here.

Proceeding towards town, there was an army recruiting office, the Roman Catholic Church of the Immaculate Conception (and school) and, after New Writtle Street, where Eastern National Head Office was situated, lived doctors Storrs and Platts, both surgeons who operated in Chelmsford and Essex Hospital next door.

A Baptist chapel here was next to yet another surgeon, Dr Corner. After more private houses and various businesses, including L M Linn & Son (Lionel & Jack), plus the Christian Science Reading Room, there was an opening to a walk along the river, which led to a footbridge into the Recreation Ground. On re-crossing the Iron Bridge in London Road, the first house by the riverside was Dr Whitley's, adjoining Councillor Fred Kearsley's dental surgery. The Inland Revenue, Chelmsford Club and Coote and Warren, coal merchants were among the offices along here.

At James Dace & Son, the music shop, one could buy a gramophone record or a grand piano, hire a pianist or have a mandolin re-strung, from proprietor Mr E W Dace. Mr Peter Bush did not take over the shop until the mid-thirties. Several changes took place along this stretch - Arthur Davies, a music teacher and Sidney Thomson a dentist, were once here and in Leys Yard, at the rear, two signwriters and Cedric Arnold, who built church organs carried on their trade. There were also a fishmongers, The Little Tindal Café, A F White, estate agent and the Misses Thorne, ladies' hairdressers. Cleale & Hadler's motorcycle and bicycle showroom was on the corner of Tindal Street.

Such a contrast to the London Road of today.

WALTON AND THE OLD LAUNDRY

In 1970, my nineteen-year-old daughter, Jennifer announced that she was going to Denmark and Norway, packed a rucksack and was off next day. How different from young people's holidays in the thirties!

In the spring, my mother would spend a day at Walton-on-Naze, finding suitable accommodation for us all, unless our stay the previous year had been perfectly satisfactory, in which case, a letter of confirmation that we would be coming again sufficed. We stayed at the same private house for about five consecutive holidays, enjoying bed, breakfast, midday meal and a light supper, every day. We also hired the same red and white striped beach hut, on the promenade not far from the pier, rather sparsely equipped with a tea service and two deck chairs. Kettles were heated on a little methylated spirits stove and we often ate fresh, locally caught shrimps for tea. The Estate Office manager, Charlie Brooker, kindly provided boiling water at teatime if one took a kettle or jug along to his centrally located office.

On the Saturday of departure for Walton, we tumbled out of bed at 4 am and were taken to the railway station by taxi, to catch the morning 'paper train', which stopped at every station, to deliver newspapers brought from London. The purpose behind this early start was to avoid the hordes of other holiday- makers, who would crowd trains later in the day. We excitedly arrived at our destination by seven o'clock, had refreshments in a café and soon after mid-day joined other regulars opening up their huts. Warm greetings were exchanged and we couldn't wait to renew old friendships. Many other Essex and London families whom we met there during the same two weeks of August, for sixteen years, became lifelong friends. In 1920, The Walton August Visitors Association had been formed by a group of annual visitors and it flourished until 1939, being reformed after the war, members organising children's sports, concerts and several other social activities - but that's another story (published in *Essex Countryside*, August 1984.). We supported the local carnival, in aid of the RNLI, several regulars having brought fancy dress from home, in anticipation.

For a week before our departure, mother would lay freshly washed and ironed clothes for us all on chairs in the front room, ready for Dad to pack, while he brought out his long green cricket bag, in which to place bats, putting clubs (for games of clock golf on the beach), shrimping nets and spades. My metal spade had already been rubbed down and painted, ready for digging on the sands. Carter Paterson, at their office in Rosebery Yard, Springfield Road, had been requested to collect our large trunk (plus two beach chairs) on the Wednesday before departure, for delivery to the railway station and onward to our accommodation in Walton. This would contain the family's clothes for our two-week stay.

Whereas today holidays are essentially mostly casual, in the thirties we took our best attire, including ties (which meant we also needed collar studs and spare collars) to wear when we visited the theatre, either on the pier, or at Clacton. White flannels were *de rigeur* for beach cricket. But black and white photographs of the era show us all ready for the water, clad in body length swimming costumes, knitted by my mother! Other photos depict my father on the beach wearing jacket and tie and he, like many other men over fifty, never bared his chest in public.

Walton pier, the second longest in the country (exceeded only by Southend) boasted its own theatre seaside troupe, led by grey-haired Auntie Ida - except that the lady reincarnated one year as bubbly blonde Ida Katrina! One of the performers was handsome German singer, Carl Shaffer, whose speciality was the popular song of the time, 'When I Grow to Old to Dream'. By 1938, the show had been renamed *The New Follies.* The theatre was not a permanent building, but a large marquee, with the sides strengthened to withstand seaside weather.

Afternoon entertainment for children was provided in the there by ventriloquist 'Clown Sunshine', and when he announced that a prize could be won by the child who came up on stage and best operated his dummy, I wanted to try. After instruction on how to work the mouth and remembering a saying often repeated by my father, I recited, in my best imitation ventriloquist's voice, "I've not been early of late and am rather backward in coming forward - I've always been behind before, but now I'm first at last!" The audience voted me best performer and I won a small bedroom clock.

There was occasionally a pianist at the Sea-Spray Restaurant at the pier entrance who entertained diners- and parents often went there for coffee after swimming. It was here, on the small stage where the Visitors' Association put on their annual concert before the pier theatre was constructed.

A penny arcade opposite was open all day. There were then no pin-tables with patterns of flashing lights, but many simple wall mounted machines, operated just by pressing a lever, to send a steel ball racing around and usually disappearing in a 'lose' cavity, very seldom in 'win' - and when it did, we simply got the penny back, ready to put back in the hungry slot and inevitably lose. There was a punch-bag machine for athletic types to show off their strength and a horse racing game, which needed six volunteers to turn, handles to make their horse go faster, before an attendant would set it in motion. When the race was over, the winner received a bar of chocolate and the man in charge often used to delight young participants by asking, "Did you try hard?" before handing out consolation small sticks of rock. That question remained a family saying for ever-more, reminding us of those happy far off days. There was one more notable game - Skeeball - where one rolled wooden balls at speed down a track, so as to bounce them up into target rings and achieve a winning score. Another arcade and café were at the far end of the pier.

Every year throughout the thirties, we would see a man at low tide on a beach beside the pier, which was not easily accessible from the high promenade, therefore mostly deserted, making a large drawing on the sand, underneath which he had scrawled, "WALTON CHURCH WITH ONE EYE". His jacket was spread out to catch any pennies that might be thrown down from the prom by passers-by and next day he would have to start all over again, after tides had inevitably destroyed his careful work. Ever after, when we drove to the resort and saw the church in the distance, someone would be bound to say, "There's Walton church with one eye!" That poor, half-blind sand artist has never been forgotten.

Another familiar sight was that of a photographer who daily stood in front of the Pier Hotel, snapping families and couples as they walked down a slope from the town and residential area to the promenade. Next day the black and white pictures, in a strip of four, would be on display in the window of Puttnam's, a photographic shop in the High Street. Regular visitors built up a collection of these holiday mementoes, which became a historical record of a family growing up, as the photographer was in his familiar position for several years.

Well established and familiar shops, such as Blue House Dairy, where we daily bought our milk, seldom changed hands and, in those days there was a large lake, adjoining the backwaters not far from the High Street, with rowing and sailing boats for hire - "Come in number eighteen" - while there were paddle boats for youngsters in a separate enclosure.

In 1933, a comedy duo known as Scott and Whaley were seen on the prom being filmed for a feature entitled *The Kentucky Minstrels*. The format was of a seaside concert party performing on a stage set up on the beach. There was a programme on the wireless with this title - forerunner of the *Black and White Minstrels* - produced by Harry S Pepper, during which, after a song and before the next 'turn', a compère would say, "Gentlemen, be seated," to be followed by furious shaking of tambourines. Some friends and I were asked to take part as extras in the film and when it came to the Regent seven months later, my parents suggested that, instead of providing a birthday party, they would pay for me to take a few pals to see it. We waited with growing excitement in anticipation of my appearance, but of course that scene had been cut!

One special enjoyment of the holiday was having occasional trips in a motorboat, *Fiona*, owned by Jonas 'Curly' Oxley, coxswain of the local lifeboat. This weather-beaten local character also used his boat daily to inspect his lobster pots and empty them of their catch. Would-be trippers, tightly clutching their sixpence fee, queued on a wide stone breakwater, which was often awash when the boat returned around high tide time.

A memorable outing, costing half a crown, which I took in *Fiona* along with eleven other passengers, the maximum complement, was to a lighthouse on the Gunfleet Sands, nine miles off shore. Jonas was a very experienced sailor, the old, two-stroke engine did not fail us - and I was given the lighthouse keepers' mail to post - but would such a journey be undertaken today, without lifejackets, in such a light, open craft?

Boat trips were also possible from the end of the pier, by paddle steamers plying between Clacton and Felixstowe and a visit to the working engine room was permitted, where an engineer was often to be seen oiling the huge pistons and other working parts. Larger ships took passengers on day outings to France and Belgium from Clacton pier and we went from there to Dunkirk in 1937 and Calais the following year, aboard the MV *Queen of the Channel*. Every time the vessel tied up, or left port her signature tune 'Lillibulero' would be relayed over loudspeakers on board. Perhaps it was played to the thousands of weary, shattered troops she rescued from the familiar waters of Dunkirk, when she played a valuable part in the 1940 evacuation, just three years after our visit.

Unlike today, when there is a continuous promenade between Walton and Frinton the two resorts were separated by red, crumbling cliffs, which we used to enjoy climbing, especially when there was an empty, derelict house to explore as it stood perilously to the cliff top. Several such homes eventually toppled over into the sea, as did the original railway lines, before the track was relocated two hundred yards further inland, but the old rails were still visible, under mounds of weeds, in the mid-thirties. Frinton was then a 'no fish and chips, caravans or pubs' town and anyone playing on the beautifully kept greensward above the beach huts, might be asked to desist. Vehicles entering the town by road first had to cross level crossing gates and this was thought to be an effective way of keeping out the day-trippers and coaches, who went on to Walton.

On our return to Chelmsford, we swapped holiday stories with friends, especially those who had also been to Walton, which has two separate holiday areas, The Naze and the pier, or Frinton end, separated by Albion beach, often thronged with day trippers. While the Naze and Albion beaches were not completely covered by the sea at high tide, the pier end was, in parts up to twelve feet deep, at which time, holidaymakers found other distractions. Walton was a popular destination, only forty-four miles away from Chelmsford and cheap Continental holidays had not then arrived.

Another annual trip the family took was to see my father's sister, in North London, where she lived in an old, three-storey house that was also her business - a hand laundry. In the tiny front garden stood an antiquated, three-wheeled pushcart, with which a man was employed to deliver baskets of clean laundry to other large houses in the district, where maids and servants were required to wear starched white collars and cuffs. This was a service in which the laundry excelled.

The front downstairs room was lined with shelves full of parcels awaiting delivery and at the end of the hall was the washroom, where two large coppers were encased in concrete, each with a coke fire below. Beside them were stools for ladies to stand on, when emptying the boilers, using galvanised hand bowls. In a corner was a washing machine, operated by turning a handle that drove a flywheel at one side. Heavy mangles with wooden rollers and worn washboards standing in baths were on tables stained with Reckitt's Blue, so completing the equipment in here, though there was also a brown earthenware sink, where we all washed, there being no bathroom in the house.

In an outhouse was a magnificent contraption for pressing sheets, eight feet long, in solid, polished mahogany. When a wheel at one side was turned, a coffin-like box, full of heavy stones moved back and forth on rollers, smoothing the sheets. On the first floor was the main ironing room and in the centre of it an eight-sided stove, fuelled by coke, was where several flat irons rested on ledges while they heated up ready for use by lady employees. There was no electricity and the rooms were lit by gas - when a jet was ignited, there was a loud 'pop' and the delicate mantle began to glow immediately. Gas mantles, mostly made by Veritas, were supplied suspended in tiny individual cartons and cost fourpence ha'penny each, or 4/3d for a box of 12.

In a sitting room upstairs was a piano, the top adorned with stuffed birds under domed glass cases but there were two other attractions we did not have at home - a wind-up gramophone and a harmonium, which was a miniature organ, with two foot pedals to pump air through the pipes. Great fun to play on, even though my repertoire did not extend much past God Save the King and Drink to Me Only with thine Eyes

Part of the enjoyment in going to London was to ride in a tram. Not far from my aunt's house brown coloured trams would hurtle down a hill, scattering a cloud of sand to maintain grip on the shiny rails before screeching to a halt as it came to our stop. Inside was a very prominent warning notice – 'No Spitting. Penalty £5'. It was a lot of money in that era, enough to deter anyone. Seats were of wooden slats and the driver stood in an open fronted cab, firmly grasping two control levers, while under one foot was a pedal he stamped on to ring a loud warning bell. At the end of the track the conductor used a long pole to move the overhead contact arm on to the opposite power line and seat backrests were reversed for the return journey. He also often had to use the pole at road junctions, when the tram changed direction and the arm needed to be relocated on crossing power lines.

It was on one of these visits that we saw Belisha Beacons for the first time, for, when the Minister of Transport, Leslie Hoare-Belisha introduced them in 1934, there was no location in Chelmsford where it was considered a necessity that a pedestrian crossing should be installed. On yet another occasion we roller skated at Alexandra Palace, in a rink which would one day be converted into BBC television studios.

Another novelty, not to be missed, was when we took a ride in the Undergound, first having negotiated escalators. It may not have been much of a thrill to the thousands who commuted by 'tube' every day, but it was a most exciting adventure for us, when we delighted in following our journey on the maps above our heads, with the added knowledge that there would be more 'moving staircases' to enjoy. An occasional treat, during my younger years, was an outing to Regent's Park Zoo, with perhaps a ride on an elephant, travelling there by a red London General bus - and a visit to a Lyons Corner House (restaurant) with a 'Nippie', clad in black dress, white apron and lacy headband to serve us, was also usually part of the fun.

FROM KEGS TO ARP

An additional feature of the entrance examination to King Edward VI Grammar School (KEGS) and Chelmsford County High School, both in Broomfield Road, was a scholarship that had been endowed many years ago, known as the Ann Johnson. 'Bright' boys and girls sat an additional exam in Victoria Road School and the pupil gaining top marks received a bursary of five pounds.   It was awarded once a year and was announced in the local press. Although the exam was taken at age eleven, the term 'eleven plus' was then unknown.

When the Technical School was opened in 1936, examinees were not offered a choice of either Tech. or Grammar school and it was unfortunately assumed, for some years, that those not quite good enough for the latter would be sent to the Tech. - whether or not their actual ability warranted it.

At the Grammar School, new pupils soon found that life was very different from what they had been used to at Council school. Teachers were now called masters and even lady teachers addressed as 'sir'. Corporal punishment, in the form of six swipes on the hand or backside (it was rumoured that boys anticipating a whacking inserted an exercise book in their trousers, to lessen the blow) from the headmaster's cane, was not unknown, while form masters had their own peculiar methods of maintaining order.   One used to haul a boy out of his seat by taking hold of his 'sideburns' - quite short hair was in vogue and there was not much of it by the ears - while another, when provoked, would walk down an aisle between desks and flail the tattered tails of his black gown at boys on either side.   This always caused amusement, which did not improve the man's anger! All masters wore black gowns and some also mortar-boards.

Having been Headmaster for nineteen years, Thomas Hay was succeeded in 1928 by 'Bill' Bailey, but he was asked to resign after five years, following some scandal. Senior boys, aware of the facts, ran an effigy of the Head to the top of the school flagpole! Prior to the appointment of old boy and sometime master Norman Squier to the headship in 1934, the Assistant Head, George W Baker had taken office as Acting Head. His nickname was 'Dickum', brought about by his habit of saying "Um" fairly regularly. Late in life, he married Mrs. Hance, widowed mother of Harold and Stanley Hance, and they lived in Cedar Avenue, in a property adjoining the school grounds.

Mr Baker's attractive daughter was the school secretary, until she married senior master Mr Findlay and was then succeeded by Mr Squier's buxom daughter, Dorothy. Another marriage involving a member of staff was that of Cecil Jones, who had been courting Gladys Butcher, a lady who for years portrayed the Virgin Mary in St Peter's Players' Nativity plays.

Boys had to wear caps when out of doors and doff them when passing a master. The penalty for not so doing could be an after school detention. Black school caps had different coloured stars on the top, according to which 'house' the boy was in - red for Tindal, blue for Holland, yellow was Mildmay and Strutt, green. Prefects had a white star, instead of a house colour. The system was changed in 1935, all caps then being identical, black with a red embroidered school badge at the front and prefects became identified by a red tassel attached to the button on the crown.

Pupils formerly at Council schools now found themselves sitting in individual desks, in 'forms' of thirty, not 'classes' of fifty and had 'break', in the 'quad', not 'playtime' in the 'playground'. Some of the older desks had former pupils' initials carved on them, often with dates from the early twenties. Form rooms were equipped with wide blackboards permanently fixed to the wall, instead of merely being on an easel and no longer did a class teacher take every subject, there was a specialist master for each - and they all had a nickname. 'Copper' Smith took Geography, (he could draw a map without looking at the blackboard), 'Pussy' Johnson, who habitually wore a bow tie and was thus frequently caricatured on blackboards, came for History, 'Egg-face' Beckett taught Latin, George 'Sarky' Purvis had his own unique - and successful - method of instilling Maths into us, 'Bruiser' Findlay was Physics master and very sweet Connie (her real name) Alderton was Art mistress. Masters were well aware of their nicknames!

When Queen Mary passed along Broomfield Road, on the way to visit her friends, the Tufnell family at 'Langleys', Great Waltham, in 1938, the whole school turned out to line the pavement and cheer. Well, not quite the whole school, for Mr Beckett decided that his form, 4a, would be far better employed taking extra Latin - a move that hardly endeared him to his pupils!

Each morning, the Rev 'Sally' Burton conducted prayers for the whole school, gathered in the Hall and French master H W 'Bill' Brooke played the organ for hymns. At the back of the stage, a stained glass window depicting such luminaries as Chaucer, Milton, Nelson and Shakespeare, had a motto scrolled on the wall above – 'Lives Of Great Men All Remind Us We Can Make Our Lives Sublime', presumably to encourage pupils in accomplishing similar heights of great achievement.

The Rev. Burton was our English master, who, with feet up on his desk, often told us jokes, sometimes organising debates and mock trials. He insisted that, in our essays, the word 'and' should not be preceded by a comma, a practice largely ignored these days, as is his other precept, that 'unique' should never be limited by an adverb, such as 'almost', 'quite' or 'absolutely'. Some teachings are never forgotten!

Particularly keen on Shakespeare, he took a party of us, in May 1939, to the Winter Garden Theatre, in London, to see *Macbeth*, with Bernard Archard as Malcolm and Robert Atkins in the title role and was preparing a full-scale school production of *The Merchant of Venice* when war broke out and the project was cancelled. The Winter Garden no longer exists; it has been replaced by the New London Theatre.

Although we could joke with masters, even pull their legs, I do not remember anyone actually being rude or cheeky to them - they were respected and most returned that respect. Wednesday afternoons were entirely devoted to optional sporting activities, but pupils had to attend school for lessons on Saturday mornings until 12.15 pm.

PT - known simply as 'drill' at Council school - was no longer mostly just arm and running exercises, but took place in a gymnasium, where masses of equipment were available for our use and we had communal shower baths to follow. 'Gym' was supervised by Maurice Bucknall, who was so well liked that he had no nickname. His wife taught piano playing and they had a large family, including two boys at the school, Mike and Pat.

Pupils were always made most welcome if they should visit their home in Main Road, Broomfield.

One of the most appreciated facilities was a tuck shop, where jam doughnuts and Chelsea buns were a penny each and a liquorice stick or Cadbury's chocolate bar cost a ha'penny. It quickly became a magnet for my threepence a week pocket money!

Fee-paying Juniors started school in a former large house, along Broomfield Road, known as Westfields, which was separated from the main school by a copse and playing field. One mistress, Miss Veysey, married tall senior master J C Corby in 1935 and then left the school. Close to Westfields house, which was demolished long ago, was a cottage, in which lived groundsmen Harry and Joe Sweeting, responsible for keeping the extensive grounds of the school ship-shape.

There were also two forms here for 11-year-olds who had passed the entrance exam, some of whom were taught by 'Tusker' Lee, a Cambridge 'half-blue'. Major Frank M Powley, who took RI (Religious Instruction) was junior school head and one day married French and singing teacher Miss (Ma) Brown, who drove to school from her home off Roxwell Road in a shiny black Austin Seven, occasionally picking up a pupil she saw walking along. Mr Powley was often called upon as prompter for Chelmsford Operatic shows at the Regent. In the main school building, facing Broomfield Road, a few boys lived as boarders during term time.

In their second year, boys were given options on which subjects they wished to take, but the choice was very limited. Anyone choosing Art would then also have to take Latin and drop History and Geography, which seems a bit hard on those who would have excelled at both Art and Geography, for instance. Boys opting for Art went into A forms, the others were in B and, somewhat miraculously, the numbers in each form evened out.

Tom Wright was German master and also formed a school orchestra, while Cecil Jones took Chemistry - first, in very old and dilapidated laboratories, replaced by new labs in 1937, which then provided a Bunsen burner and running water facilities for each student. Making a dreadful stink in there with sulphuretted hydrogen (similar to rotten eggs) was a lingering achievement.

'Nobby' Squier introduced a new style of term reports, in book form, instead of their being on individual sheets of paper. Masters - and parents - could then easily refer back to previous ones, to check on progress, or, more likely ascertain how often "could do better" appeared !

Every summer, we enjoyed eight weeks holiday, in place of the six weeks we had previously known at Council school. This helped to make up for evenings spoiled by having to do homework! Boys who were in the cadet corps turned up once a week in their khaki uniforms, including puttees, which laboriously had to be wound around each leg and they had 'field days', taking part in army style manoeuvres. In a field behind the main school were 'the butts' where shooting practice could sometimes be heard taking place. The cadet band, more correctly known as the Corps of Drums, were given their smart red uniforms in 1936, by Mrs Lavinia Keene, of Galleywood and the first-rate drum and bugle band, complete with a drum major who regularly tossed his mace high in the air, was in much demand at shows and carnivals throughout Essex, being efficient both in smart appearance and tuneful performance.

There were two venues for sports activities, the fields beside the school and Newfields, along the road towards Broomfield, close to the Girls' High School, both being marked out with several football and hockey pitches. Proximity to the girls did not mean they collaborated in sporting activities, but it was not unknown for boys to wait outside their school for a girlfriend to emerge! When this came to the ears of headmistress Miss Cadbury, she had the practice stopped. Some girls then waited opposite the Grammar School, until that, too was forbidden. But love will find a way and the problem was resolved by keeping their tryst on the steps of the Library, in Duke Street, which had been built in 1935.

Very distinctive blazers, for wearing to cricket or on sports days, teamed with white flannels, had wide red and black stripes. School ties were in similar colours, but with more discreet, narrow red stripes on black. The excellent school motto, translated from Latin, declared, 'Whatever thy hand findeth to do, do it with all thy might'. In other words 'if you are going to do a job, do it properly'. Well worth remembering when tackling some DIY at home!

A roller skating rink, in London Road, opposite the hospital, was owned by Mr Hickley, one time town councillor, who also owned the Select Cinema (they were adjacent) and lived nearby. It had a wooden floor and the noise of metal wheels from dozens of skates, accompanied by amplified Souza music, could be quite deafening. Several grammar school boys enjoyed skating there regularly on Saturday afternoons and a school hockey team was formed, with Mr Hickley's approval. There were five in a team and they played against those from other skating rinks, for a couple of years, until the team was disbanded when boys left school.

The Rialto dance band, was also formed at the school and played at various town venues. Later, it re-formed as the Harlem Knights band, members being Bernard and Ken Fox, Laurie Osborn and Laurie Rocker. It was very popular for the strength of its music, in much demand by dancegoers. It easily matched the quality of other local bands, like Altona and Bert Barneveld's Barney's Band, which had of more mature musicians. In the late twenties, another popular band in the town was The Chelma Five.

Before the era of GCSEs and A-Levels, fifth form students were able to gain School Certificate in various subjects. A pupil achieving five of these had Matriculated and received an additional certificate. Nowadays, there is no space on job application forms for such achievements! Boys who stayed on in the sixth form studied for Higher School Certificate and other exams, many going on to university.

Many former pupils were recognised well-known traders in the town and others achieved notable success in later life, more than one reaching the rank of Major General, or becoming chairmen of major companies. Some joined the Diplomatic Corps and became High Commissioners, while during the war; at least two were outstanding RAF fighter aces. Brian Parkyn was an MP in the mid-thirties and Conservative Government Minister, Sir Norman Fowler, was at the school in the forties, while Mike Smith's name is recognised as a prominent Disc Jockey on the radio.

On one day during the week following my family's last ever summer holiday at Walton-on-Naze, in August, 1939, my school pal Adrian and I cycled the forty-four miles there, to retrieve a book I had left behind in the boarding house. On the way home in the dark, my front lamp failed as we passed Henry Ford's mansion at Boreham and this seemed to us to confirm rumours that a secret ray was being tried out in that area! War was imminent and we clutched at any stories of weapons that would be used to help us defeat Hitler. I cycled the rest of the way behind Adrian and replaced the bulb next day, convinced that the mysterious ray had put it out.

Early in 1939, an appeal had been made for young men, who owned a bicycle, to volunteer as ARP messengers and a few, including myself, enrolled. For several weeks, trainee personnel attended regular lectures, given by Major Doe MC, at the Coval Lane Health Clinic. We learned about wearing gas masks, the functions of Air Raid Wardens and procedures to follow should war break out. Then a couple of us were assigned to duties in the basement of County Hall, where several lady telephonists manned switchboards. The room was almost below Duke Street and in fact had an 'escape hatch' into the street, so, if a bomb had fallen in the vicinity, the command centre could have easily been wiped out - not very good planning! We were all there on duty at 11 am on the morning of 3rd September and heard Neville Chamberlain's fateful broadcast.

Thus ended the peaceful life enjoyed in Chelmsford. However had we managed all those previous years, without a fridge-freezer, television, mobile phone, sliced bread, frozen chips, instant showers and even plastic bags? Perhaps the lack of them had contributed to that peace.

Abraham, A J 59
Adams, Douglas 21
Adams, Violet 20
Admirals Park 27,34,36,47,51
Aitken, Sister 54
Alderton, Connie 71
Alford, Miss C M 46
Alford, Dr C W 12,38,40,43
All Saints 8,21,53
Amey & Cook 11,15
Anchor pub 60
Andrews, Arthur 10,46
Angel Yard 18
Arbour Lane 63
Armitage, Miss 6
Army & Navy 59
Arnold, Cedric 64
Ascension Church 53
Ashdown's buses 39
Ashford, Miss 16
Austin, John 10
Back Street 17
Baddow Road 23,26,30,38,39,59
Bailey, Bill 70
Baker, George W 70
Baker, PC 16
Bancroft, Miss F M 3
Baptist Church 12
Barclay's Bank 16
Barford, George 1
Barn pub 8
Barneveld, Bert 73
Barrack Square 26
Barrow, Canon 20
Beach Drive 47
Backett, Egg-face 71
Beehive Lane 31,55
Bell Hotel 18
Bellamy family 1,15,63
Betts, T 59
Billington, F R 6,8
Bishopscourt 63
Black Boy 63
Black Bull 28
Blooman, G C 3
Bluebird restaurant 2
Blyth, Mr 35
Boarded Barns 3,51,53
Bocking, Cecil 20
Bolingbroke, Stanley 16,22,26,63
Bond, J G 3,22,61
Boreham, Charles 59
Bouverie Road 5
Britton, J E 46
Brooke, H W 71
Broomfield Hospital 31

Broomfield Road 1,3-5,14,31,51,71-2
Brown, Miss 62,72
Brownings Avenue 3,38
Bucknall, Maurice 72
Budd, W & O 1,59,62,63
Bunn, Early 24
Burdon, Percy 30
Burgess Well Road 46
Burrell, Frank 24
Burton, Sally 71
Bush, William P 37,52,64
Butcher, Gladys 70
Byford, Frank 10
Cadbury, Miss 73
Caper, Sidney 46
Cass, H H 26
Cass, Phyllis 52
Cathedral Hall 11,20
Cathedral School 11
Catling, Harold 59
Caton, Albert 24
Caton, Misses 17
Catt, Ralph 59,63
Cawley, A J 4
Cedar Avenue 4,37,46,70
Cedar Café 10
Chaplin, Charlie 27
Chaplin, J C 24
Chelmer & Blackwater 62
Chelmsford Gaol 62
Chelmsford … Hospital 31,43,64
Chelmsford AODS 20,23,57,72
Chelmsford City FC 33,35
Cheyne, Mrs 17
Christy, Leonard F 51
Christy Bros 4,51
Christy & Norris 51
Clarke, J H 25
Clarkson, Thomas 38,41,54
Clist, Leonard F 7
Cobb & Wincer 11,12
Cole, E K 55
Collier, Broom 63
Collins, Jack 62
Compasses Inn 4
Congregational Church 59,63
Cook, Miss 6
Coombs, Mrs 60
Co-operative Stores 8,22,26,59,63
Corby, J C 72
Corey, Mr 6
Corn Exchange 13,15,21
Corner, Dr 64
Cottee, Miss M E 11
Cottom, E R 16
Council Offices 1

County High School 3,5,70
County Hotel 46
Coval Lane 39,46,74
Cowan, J 63
Cramphorn's 1,16,17,22,60,63
Crane Court 16,21
Crees, Tom 32
Crompton's 31,54
Currie, R H 5,8
Cutts, Audrey 20
Cutts, Mr 26
Dace, James 52,64
Dannatt, Mr 12
Darby, Alfred 24
Davies, Arthur 64
Dawson, Mrs 41
Day, John E 46
Denoon, Donald 36,39,46
Dick, Miss 6
Dixon, Alderman 11
Doe, Major 74
Dolphin 17,18
Double, Mr 60
Drill Hall 12
Duffield, Edna 63
Duke Street 1,2,10,15,18,26,31,38
Dutton, John 18,24
Eastern Garages 12
Eastern National 1,13,23,38,39
Eaton, Frank 46
Empire Theatre/Cinema 56,62
Escott, Ronald 13,36
Essex Arms 63
Essex Chronicle 24
Essex Home School 34,37
Evans, Ernie 60
Everett, Daddy 44
Fairbrass, Mr 60
Fairfield Road 1
Fairhead, Ted 2,16
Fewell, John 32
Fincham, Walter H 59,60
Findlay, Bruiser 70,71
First Avenue 3
Fish, Reginald 20,34
Foreman, L P 39,47
Fourth Avenue 3
Fowler, Norman 74
Fox, Bernard & Ken 73
Fox, Mr 26
Frear, Harold 60
French, Fred J 17,46
French, R E 60
Friars School 5,61
Fulcher, Percy 11
Fyffe, Monte 55

Gard, J 59
Gibson, G H 61
Gifford, Leonard 21
Glebe Road 3
Godfrey, H & T C 12,15,60
Golden Fleece 12,13
Golden Lion 18
Goldsmith, Mr 26
Gramlick, C J 1,46
Gray, Ernest C 59
Green, Peggy 20,21
Grew, T H 60
Grey-Green coaches 40
Gripper, Joseph 16
Grove Road 60
Guy Harlings 15
Hadler, Bob 12
Hall Street 56,60
Hamlet Road 60
Hance, Stanley & Harold 17,46,70
Harknett, Mrs G 32
Harris, Dr 36
Harris, Walter 10
Harrison, H J 11
Hart, Cecil 46
Harvey, George 1,10
Hasler & Hance 17,18
Hawkes 1,10,11,23,63
Hawkes, G J 37
Hawkes, Jack 46
Hay, Thomas 70
Heard, Margery 11
Henry Road 42
Hickley, Mr 73
High Street 1,5,15-17,22-26,31,38,62
Hilliard, G B 15,16
Hillman, Ernest 39,40
Hiner family 3
Hoffmans 3,31,51,54,55
Holberton, Eileen 60
Holmes, Don 4
Holy Trinity Church 62
Hopkirk, Revd 62
Houghton, Cliff 11
Howes, Tommy 59
Hoy, Harry 1
Hunt, E L 26
Hutchinson, Mr 62
Hymas, Mr 7
Ireland, Misses 36
Jacobs, Major 46
Jeffkins, Miss 62
Johnson, Pussy 46,71
Johnson, W J 3
Jones, Billy 23
Jones, Cecil 70,72

Jones, Mr 6
Jordan, John 10
Judge, Cecil 24
Kearsley, Fred 64
Keene, John H 3
Keene, Lavinia 3,73
King, A C 46
King Edward Avenue 13,33
King Edward School 4,13,70
King's Road 3,4,27,51
King's Road School 5,6,7,8,38
Kingcome, Mrs 46
Lady Lane 5
Lee, Tusker 72
Levett, Laurie 24
Levett, Nellie 8
Leys Yard 64
Library 12,73
Ling, G B 17,46
Linn, Lionel & Jack 64
Lion & Lamb 10
Lloyd's Bank 25
Lodge's coaches 39
London Road 5,16,17,39,52,63,73
Longstomps Avenue 5
Lower Moulsham 5
Luckin & Sheldrake 15
Macklin, Madge 20
Macpherson, James 11
Maguire, Mr 62
Maltese Road 28,37,53
Manor Road 5
Marconi 1,4,31,54,55,56
Market House 18,24
Market Road 10,12-3,18,31,38-9,54
Marriage, Misses 3
Marriage's Mill 59
Marsh, Mr 7
Martin, Dr 3,46
Mason, Joan 52
Mason, Joseph 10,61
Mather, Geroge W 11
McNair, Mrs 17
Medley, Harry 35
Mellor, Miss 6
Merritt, Tom 16
Methodist Church 23,37
Midland Bank 24
Mildmay Road 5,59
Monk, Leonard 2
Moon, Alec O 6,8
Morgan, J H 8
Morgan, Michael 30
Morgan, Mrs 52
Morrish, R G 31,33
Morrow, W E R 15

Mossman, Jean 21
Moulsham Street 5,13,23,31,38,39,59
Moy, Thomas 18
Mullocks, Miss 60
Munnion, Freddy 20,21
Murdoch, Nelson 23
Nag's Head 59
National Provincial Bank 24
Navigation Road 62
New London Road 25,60
New Street 3,11,15,31,54
New Writtle Street 61,63
Newton, Dr 1
Norton Road 35
Orchard Street 60
Orrin, George 60
Osborn, Laurie 73
Outten, Mr 37
Page, George 37
Parfitt, Tom 34
Park Avenue 5,27,30,41,43,47,51
Park Road 12,32
Parkins, Owen & Harold 37
Parkyn, Brian 74
Parrett, Audrey 20
Pash, J Brittain 14,46
Passfield, Mr 47,51
Patching Hall Lane 4,39
Pavilion Cinema 46,56
Payne, E N 1
Payne, W J 3
Pease, Leonard 20
Perry, Cecil 17
Petchey, Jack 18
Phillips, Maurice 20
Pigg, Harry 63
Pitts, R E 63
Plough 2
Poney, Frank 60
Poney, Fred 17
Pope & Smith 17
Pope, Dudley 17
Porter, Mr 47
Potter, Henry 1
Powley, Frank M 72
Preston, Warwick 61
Primrose coaches 39
Primrose Hill 36,44,51
Pryke, J C 37
Purvis, George 71
Queen Street 38,60
Queen's Head 26
Radcliffe, Miss M E 63
Railway Street 3
Railway Tavern 12
Rainsford End 5,23

Rainsford House 1
Rainsford Lane 34-36
Rainsford Road 28,31,35-6,43,51
Raven, Bert 16
Read, Miss 6
Recreation Ground 12,13,32,64
Rectory Lane 3,31,54
Red Lion 63
Regent Theatre 23,39,72
Ridley, C E 3,63
Rippingale, Ted 8
Rippon, Alan 1,46
Rippon, E J 16
Rising Sun 64
Rison, Mrs 24
Ritz Cinema 24,56,57,59
Rocker, Laurie 73
Rodd, Doris 21,63
Rose & Crown 37
Rose Bros 10
Rosebery Hotel 63
Rosebery Yard 65
Rowe, Ralph 46
Rowland, Ernest 37
Roxwell Road 39,47,51,72
Russell, Maidie 21
Russell, Percy 20,21
Ryder, George 59
Sadd, John 59
Sainsbury, John J 24
St Anne's School 64
St Cedd's School 37
St John's Hospital 3,31
St John's School 60
St Margaret's School 63
St Peter's 8,17,44,47,51
St Peter's School 36,53
St Phillip's Priory 64
Salvation Army 60
Sandford Road 62
Saracen's Head 16,18
Saunders, Gilbert 24
Scarlet, Mr 15
School View Road 37
Scotch Wool Shop 16,22
Select Cinema 56,73
Self & Hicks 16
Sellick, Mr 36
Sergeant, John 46
Seventh Avenue 3

Shakeshaft, Mr 8
Shedd, Misses 1
Shedd, Mr 1
Shemming, F W 37
Shergold, H G 10
Ship Inn 3
Shire Hall 15,54
Slaughter, Dr 63
Slipper, J Walter 11
Slythe, J B 63
Smee, Misses 60
Smith, Copper 71
Smith, Fred Luckin 3,25,26,60,63
Smith, Mike 74
Smith, Percy 10
Smith, Peter & Ray 17
Sorrell, Hilda 11
Spalding, Fred 16,46,64
Spencer, Don 17
Spotted Dog 17,18
Springfield Park Road 62
Springfield Road
5,22,26,38,39,47,56,62
Squier, Norman 70,72
Stanley, Norman 23
Star & Garter 60
Station 2,10
Stedman, Maurice 8
Steele, Jack & Harold 30
Stock, Edith 60
Stone Bridge 23,26,59
Stumps Lane 63
Sturgeon, George 8,9
Sunbeam Café 59
Sweeting, Harry & Joe 72
Swiss Avenue 4,14
Tapp, F J 24
Tappenden, Mr 7
Taylor, Fred 10
Taylor, II J 36
Taylor, Sidney C 20,36,50
Third Avenue 3
Thompson, J Ockleford 24,64
Thompson, J W 3
Thomson, Sidney 64
Thorne, Misses 64
Threadneedle Street 12,13
Three Cups 62
Tindal Café 16
Tindal Street 17,24

Tindall & Jarrold 15
Tindall Square 13,15,17,24,38,60
Tomalin, Harold 34
Torry, Gilbert & Alec 20
Tower Avenue 51
Tower Gardens 44,47,51
Tremear, J H 6,7
Trinity Road School 5,62
Tucker, Vic 34
Tuffnell family 71
Tunbridge, Frank 61
Turner, Ashley 53
Turner, Fred 14
Turner, Mrs 1
Two Brewers 62
Tye, Mr 60
Upper Bridge Road 10
Van Dieman's Road 59
Verdult, Chris 2
Vesey, Miss 72
Viaduct Road 32,46
Victoria Road 5,10,12,62,63
Wadley, Miss 6
War Memorial 1
Ward, Frank 11
Waring, Geoff 60
Warwick Square 27,51
Waterhouse Farm 36
Waterloo Lane 15
Webber, W G 11
Weight Road 62
Wells Street 2
Wenley, Robert 26,39,63
Westminster Bank 16
White, A F 64
White Hart 18
Whitley, Dr 64
Wilcocks, R W 63
Wilcox, Gilbert 12
Wilks, Tony & Mary 10
Williams, Mrs 34
Willingham, Joe 60
Wilson, H A 63
Windmill Inn 59
Wiseman, A E 11,16
Wood Street 31,59
Woodland Road 8
Wright, Hugh 2,18,61,63
Wright, Tom 72
Writtle Road 31,36,64

The author in his salad days